Silent Voices of the Soul

How to Recognize the Spiritual Messages in Everyday Life

First published by O Books, 2010
O Books is an imprint of John Hunt Publishing Ltd., The Bothy, Deershot Lodge, Park Lane, Ropley, Hants, SO24 0BE, UK
office1@o-books.net
www.o-books.net

Distribution in:

UK and Europe
Orca Book Services
orders@orcabookservices.co.uk
Tel: 01202 665432 Fax: 01202 666219
Int. code (44)

USA and Canada
NBN
custserv@nbnbooks.com
Tel: 1 800 462 6420 Fax: 1 800 338 4550

Australia and New Zealand
Brumby Books
sales@brumbybooks.com.au
Tel: 61 3 9761 5535 Fax: 61 3 9761 7095

Far East (offices in Singapore, Thailand, Hong Kong, Taiwan)
Pansing Distribution Pte Ltd
kemal@pansing.com
Tel: 65 6319 9939 Fax: 65 6462 5761

South Africa
Stephan Phillips (pty) Ltd
Email: orders@stephanphillips.com
Tel: 27 21 4489839 Telefax: 27 21 4479879

Design: Stuart Davies

ISBN: 978 1 84694 287 7

A CIP catalogue record for this book is available from the British Library.

Printed by Digital Book Print

Silent Voices of the Soul

How to Recognize the Spiritual Messages in Everyday Life

Robin Leigh Vella

Winchester, UK
Washington, USA

CONTENTS

This book is dedicated to my beautiful mother, Isis, for lighting the way to truth.

'What lies behind us and what lies before us are tiny matters compared to what lies within us.'
Ralph Waldo Emerson

Preface

You are holding a simple approach to spiritual awareness in your hands. I wrote this book for you. It is easy to read, and easy to understand. You do not need a dictionary. You will not have to backtrack. You only need to read each sentence once.

Signs and symbols are everywhere. Spiritual messages are all around you. This book not only teaches you how to become aware of them; it also shows you how to discover what they really mean. Spirit is always speaking the truth; *Silent Voices of the Soul* is about recognizing 'the whisper'.

Reading definitions of metaphysical concepts is one thing; being able to personally relate to them is another. *Silent Voices of the Soul* gently guides you into both worlds. In this book, you will find clear explanations of spiritual principles. You will also read true stories, excerpts from my own spiritual journey that show what they look like in real life.

Silent Voices of the Soul is more than an everyday guidebook. It is a collection of life-changing lessons, the things you learn as you walk the road to truth. It shows you how to have a positive running conversation with the universe. It teaches you how to create a light-filled life. It reminds you to trust your heart – to be who you really are.

Spirit whispered these life-changing lessons to me. I wrote them down. I carried them into the physical world. I learned them and used them to heal my life. For years, I have been teaching them to others. Now, it is an honor and a blessing to share them with you.

With love and peace and prayers for healing,

Robin

http://www.robinleighvella.com

Acknowledgments

My heart is filled with love and gratitude for all the souls who made this book possible. I would like to thank the following people for contributing their special gifts to this project.

John for inviting me on the adventure and loving me in ways beyond words; Jp for teaching me life-changing lessons and computer skills simultaneously; Thomas for whispering this book to me before you were born and teaching it ever since; Dad for all your loving support: spiritual and editorial; Cheryl Leisner for devoting your time and energy in so many ways: typing, formatting and editing the original manuscript; Don O'Keefe for your guidance, support and kindness, and for designing the perfect book cover; Michael Spitale for reminding me to always be who I really am; Susan Coleman for walking into the light with me.

I would also like to thank the following people for their love and support.

My sisters Dannielle Cohen and Hillary DeParde; Carolyn Luttio, Cynthia Kyle, Diane Spitale, Kathleen and Gary Centola, Marlene Nordquist, Marta O'Keefe, Robert Cooper, my wonderful clients, and Nina and Grandpa, who always send their love from the other side. Special thanks to Krista Goering, my amazing agent and angel, for your support, encouragement and guidance – for believing in this book, assisting in its transformation and placing it in a beautiful home.

Special thanks also to John Hunt, for publishing this book, and making it possible for me to realize my biggest dream. And to my Guides, the silent voices of my soul, thank you for entrusting me with this project and loving me while I was learning how to love myself.

Author Note

Soul

What is the soul? The soul is our heart of hearts – the sum total of all we are as a result of having loved and being loved. It is the energy of every life lesson we have learned in the name of love. The soul is our vibration that resonates with the universe. It is the eternal home of Spirit where we hold all our answers – all our truths.

Spirit

Spirit is our soul's voice – the unconditional, loving whisper that speaks the truth. It is our wisdom and universal knowing, the divine guidance within us that supports our Highest Good. Spirit is joy. Spirit is passion. Spirit is peace. Spirit is love. Spirit is light shining from the soul, illuminating truth to direct us to our dreams.

About the Cover

This extraordinary cover depicts one of the most powerful messages the author has ever received. Designed by artist Don O'Keefe of Lyndonville, N.Y. (http://www.donokeefe.com/coverspage.htm), it captures a moment of revelation when the truth made itself known (see chapter 7: Spiritual Transformation).

Introduction

Remember when we were signing up for this lifetime? We were standing in line together in an enormous room, registering for classes in The School for Higher Learning, choosing which courses to take and when.

There was a guidebook on the table – a gift for us. We were told to memorize it on our way out the door. It was a collection of truths our heart would hold and our soul would always know.

But the bell rang. School started. Our new life began. And the book we were supposed to bring with us suddenly disappeared. Somehow, in all the commotion, we left it behind. Or did we?

Every moment of every day, our silent voices speak to us, sharing wisdom from that invisible guidebook our soul knows by heart. Yet sometimes life is too noisy for us to hear them or fear makes us 'forget' them. So here are the words to help us remember.

Chapter 1

Recognizing the Whisper

The idea came out of nowhere. For some reason, I decided to invite my husband John out to breakfast. It was a last-minute decision, not the original plan. The kids had gone to school. John was researching stocks on the internet. I was listening to the radio, waiting for clothes to dry. Before I had a chance to think about it, I asked my husband for a date.

'I'm ready whenever you are,' he said.

I almost changed my mind on the way out the door. What was I thinking? The floor needed to be mopped. Dishes were soaking in the sink. There was a mountain of laundry on the basement floor. I didn't have time to go out to breakfast. I had work to do.

Still, something told me to get into the car.

'Where do you want to go?' John asked, as we backed out of the driveway.

'I don't care,' I said. 'Surprise me.'

We decided to take a drive while we considered our options. It was a gorgeous spring day. The sun was shining. The sky was blue. The magnolias were in full bloom.

I was admiring the scenery while we were stopped at an intersection. John was looking in a different direction.

'Rob, look down the road,' he said, interrupting my quiet moment.

The tone in his voice startled me. I immediately turned my head. Far off in the distance, I noticed the flashing lights. I looked at them and for a split second I thought of my son, Thomas. He was going on a field trip with his kindergarten class. His bus was supposed to leave at 9:30 a.m. I looked at my watch. It was 9:31 a.m.

'How close are we to Thomas's school?' I asked.

In that exact moment, my husband turned on the radio. We had tuned in late to breaking news. There had been a bus crash near my son's school. No details were available. We looked at each other without saying a word; I reminded myself to breathe.

John drove toward the flashing lights. When we reached a roadblock, I got out of the car and ran to the scene in front of me. A car was overturned. Broken glass was strewn in every direction. An ambulance and a police car were pulling away with their sirens on.

I felt sick to my stomach. My hands started to sweat; my heart started to pound.

Doing my best to breathe, I scanned my surroundings. The street looked deserted. Everything was still. I didn't see a bus. I didn't see any children. Thomas's school was nowhere in sight. For a moment I thought I was having a nightmare; I wondered when I was going to wake up.

The sound of footsteps broke the silence; I wasn't alone. A police officer was walking down the street. I ran to him.

'I just heard about the bus crash on the radio,' I said, trying to be calm. 'My son goes to that school. Were there any injuries?'

He hesitated for a moment before he spoke.

'Oh, that was a different accident,' he said, putting his hand on my shoulder to comfort me. 'All of the kids are OK.'

A tingling sensation raced through me.

'You can't imagine how much you have helped me. Thank you so much,' I said.

Filled with gratitude, I ran back to the car to give John the news. We drove away in silence. When we arrived home, I called Thomas's school to confirm what the officer had told me. The principal reassured me that everything was all right. Fifteen kindergarteners had been taken to the hospital for observation, she explained. If my son had been involved in the incident, I would have received a call. I wasn't notified because he was on a different bus.

After I spoke to the principal, I listened to my voicemail. My friend, Cindy, had left a message.

'Where are you? I have something to tell you. Please call me,' she said.

When I called her back, she asked me where I had been. My friend was worried; she had been trying to reach me all morning. Cindy knew about the bus crash. She had been watching TV. Local stations had been broadcasting special reports.

I told her that everything was all right. I explained how I discovered the truth.

'Nothing like this has ever happened to me before,' I said. 'It felt surreal – like I was an actor in a movie.'

'That police officer was an angel,' she replied. 'Thank God you decided to go out to breakfast. It's a good thing you didn't stay home.'

Cindy's words went straight to my heart. Until that moment, I hadn't considered the big picture.

Had I been home, I would have answered Cindy's call; she would have told me to turn on the TV. I would have seen a car wedged under the front of a bus. I would have heard that kindergarteners from Thomas's school had been taken to the hospital.

I would have been in a state of panic, hoping no one had been badly injured – praying that my son was OK.

After our conversation, I sat down on the couch to breathe. In quiet, my mind replayed the morning. Spirit made me aware of all the ways I had been guided to truth. My eyes filled with tears. I said 'Thank you' out loud, most grateful to have recognized the whisper.

***

Imagine: We are in a noise-filled room, waiting to receive an important message. The CD player is blasting. The television is as loud as its volume setting will allow, and everyone is shouting at each other in an effort to be heard.

Meanwhile, our messenger is knocking at the door. Unfortunately, in all the noise, we are unable to hear him. He knocks a little harder, but we are still unaware of his presence. He knocks again with all the energy he can muster, but even this attempt to attract our attention is unsuccessful. So our messenger walks away, hoping to reach us later.

Intuition is Spirit whispering from the soul. It tells us when we are living our truths; it tells us when we have strayed from our paths. It tells us which decision to make; it tells us which direction to take. Gently and quietly, it guides us to our answers. All we have to do is listen. But first we must ask ourselves, 'Are we ready to hear?'

Spirit speaks by quietly pointing us in the right direction. It continually reminds us who we are, why we are here and what we are here to do. Ready, willing and able to provide us with answers, Spirit whispers our truth to us. But sometimes the whisper is too quiet for us to recognize.

Our voice of wisdom has competition: loud, distracting 'noises' of the mind. By nature, the mind is not quiet. It creates and contains varying degrees of noise: thinking, analyzing, rationalizing, doubting, judging, fearing and debating. The list continues and each item on it is loud enough to drown out our intuition, even when Spirit is whispering as loudly as possible.

The only way to receive Spirit's messages is to be quiet enough to hear them. How do we become quiet? We eliminate the noise in our mind. In other words, we 'shut off' all mental activities such as thinking, analyzing, rationalizing, doubting, judging and fearing, until the only 'sound' we hear is silence.

Anything we can equate with peace and relaxation will enable us to create a quiet mind. Prayer, meditation, walking, cooking, dancing, writing, gardening and cleaning are some of the many ways to achieve mental stillness. The possibilities are limitless. How we make it happen is our choice.

In a quiet mind, Spirit's whisper can be recognized for what it is – intuition – our ever-present inner knowing. Intuition is the divine energy within us that guides us to our Highest Good. It leads us to our answers; we need not pose the questions. It is wisdom apart from logic and reason. Therefore we never have to ask what, when, where, how or why.

Every soul holds the gift of intuition. Every one of us is capable of hearing Spirit's voice. It does not need to be developed, because intuition is whole, complete and available to us when we are ready and willing to receive it. It requires no analysis; there is no reason to question truth. It does not need to be awakened; Spirit never sleeps.

Imagine: We are inside a storage room. It is dark, dusty and overflowing with clutter. Things we have been meaning to throw away, but are still holding onto, are scattered everywhere. Outdated files, papers yellowed with age, and other purposeless possessions litter the floor. Every available space has been occupied.

Someone else is in the room – Divine Intelligence. He (She) is holding a book titled *Answers to Life's Questions* and waves it to attract our attention. But it is impossible to see him. Too many things are blocking our view. He tries to move toward us. His attempts are futile; our old stuff is in his way. Trapped among the clutter, Divine Intelligence is unable to find us. Our answers are out of reach.

When there is so much stuff occupying our mind, it is impossible to receive intuition. Even though Divine Intelligence is always available to us, our mind must be clear in order to receive it.

Mental clutter is old, useless energy that is only taking up space. Disappointment, negative and limited thoughts, old belief systems that no longer serve us, outdated definitions of our self and our world – anything preventing us from keeping a clear, open mind falls into the clutter category.

Just as we would throw household clutter away, so must we let go of the useless energies our mind no longer needs to own. By creating 'open-mindedness', we are clearing the pathway to intuition.

There are many ways to clear mental clutter. We can visualize it disintegrating into dust and watch the wind carry it away. We can make a list of the energies we are releasing and then either tear it up and throw it out, or burn it and dispose of the ashes however we desire. Or we can envision our mind as a clean, clear, light-filled space prepared to welcome Divine Intelligence. Any of these scenarios, or one of our own design, demonstrates a readiness and willingness to receive intuition.

When the Spirit Speaks

Intuition reaches us in a calm, quiet and clear mind – before we have the opportunity to think. It is the idea that surfaces out of nowhere – our first impression of someone or something, without logic or reason to back it up. It is our inner knowing, unsupported by fact or physical evidence. It is the whisper telling us 'what is' without needing to explain 'why'.

Spirit speaks silently in the voice with many names: Divine Intelligence, Universal Knowing, the God or Goddess within, Great Spirit... Whatever we call it is our choice. Just know and always remember to trust this voice, because it always speaks the truth.

Here is a story from my own life that demonstrates why we should always listen to our intuition.

Doubting the voice

I was making my first lemon meringue pie and needed to do it as quickly as possible. Never mind that lemon pie is one of the most challenging baking projects anyone, let alone a novice, could hope to execute successfully. My mother-in-law was coming over to watch my every move. If there was a way to expedite the process, I was going to find it and I was going to use it.

The clock was ticking and there were many details to attend to: making and baking the crust, preparing the filling, and beating the meringue into stiff, dry peaks. Overwhelmed, I grabbed the necessary ingredients, attempting to make both the crust and filling simultaneously. I was becoming anxious. It wasn't until dizziness forced me to sit down that I realized I needed to breathe.

Each breath I drew helped bring me back to reality. 'This is only a pie,' I reminded myself. 'It doesn't have to be perfect,' I tried to believe. 'Slow down, relax and get a hold of yourself!' I demanded, having heard my mother's voice inside my head.

But time was running short; I needed to speed things up. My mother-in-law was due to arrive within the hour. Fortunately, I remembered I had a ready-to-bake piecrust in the freezer.

As I preheated the oven for the store-bought crust, I kept thinking that my mother, the Master Chef, would cringe if she could see me right now. Unlike her, I was unfamiliar with the crust-making procedure and now was not the time to learn. 'At least I'll be making the rest of the pie from scratch,' I rationalized, as I prepared the filling, set it on the counter to cool and slipped the crust into the oven.

My timing couldn't have been more perfect – I pulled my crust from the oven the moment my mother-in-law pulled into the driveway. Now all I needed to do was let it cool. Placing the crust on the counter next to the filling, I hurried to the front door to greet my mother-in-law.

Impatience soon called me back into the kitchen.

As far as I was concerned, things were not proceeding quickly enough. The filling had reached room temperature, but the crust was still hot to the touch. Ten more minutes on the counter and both would be cool enough to handle.

My mother-in-law had suddenly become my shadow – ten minutes seemed like forever.

I searched my mind for crust-cooling ideas. Putting it in the refrigerator for a few minutes would work, but it was too full. The freezer was a consideration, but it was fuller than the refrigerator. Then I had another thought. We frequently left pots of soup outside to cool. I could set the crust on the porch ledge for a while.

I reached for the crust, deciding to put my last thought into action. The moment I felt it in my hands, an inexplicable feeling came over me, causing me to momentarily rethink what I was about to do. There was no reason to believe that bringing the crust outside was a mistake. There was nothing factual to support my feeling. But I was reacting as if someone had just whispered, *Don't do it, Robin. You'll be sorry.*

Somewhere deep inside, I knew my intuition was attempting to redirect me. Spirit had spoken in the voice of caution. Unfortunately, in my anxiety, I mistook divine guidance for an overactive imagination, bypassing the message it was attempting to relay. Even as I picked up the crust and began walking toward the door, that same feeling accompanied me. As I opened the door, I hesitated before taking the crust outside.

One foot was in the house, the other on the porch, as I vacillated over what to do. From a logical standpoint, my indecisive behavior made no sense. There was no reason behind it. Still, nothing could explain the uneasy feeling I was trying to push aside.

A rush of arctic air finally forced me to make my decision. I was freezing and tired of over-thinking. Ignoring my intuition, I walked onto the porch, set the crust on the ledge and came back inside.

That uncomfortable feeling followed me. The moment I closed the door, I knew I had made a mistake. By the time I changed my mind, opened the door and walked back onto the porch, it was too late.

At first, I thought someone had played a practical joke on me. My crust was gone! I had only been inside for a minute; it had disappeared. As I searched the entire porch, I talked to myself.

'Who would have taken it? What could have happened to it? Where the hell did it go?' I yelled.

Spirit had tried to warn me; I was sorry that I hadn't listened. My piecrust was nowhere to be found.

Frustrated and perplexed, I sat down on the ledge to breathe the fresh air. The neighborhood was quiet and still. White fluffy clouds were drifting overhead. Naked trees stood in stark beauty against the January sky. Breathing slowly and purposefully, I allowed nature to embrace me.

In my peaceful state of being, a missing piecrust was no longer important. I didn't need to know where it was anymore. I decided to go back inside.

As I started walking toward the door, something made me turn around. For some reason, I felt compelled to look over the ledge, into the bushes below me. It wasn't long before I understood why. Wedged between them was something round, shiny and silver, reflecting light in my direction.

Walking down the porch steps, I made my way through the bushes to retrieve my upside-down pie tin. When I picked it up I discovered there was nothing underneath it.

I wondered what had happened.

On the way back to the house, Spirit whispered to me. A memory surfaced from my quiet mind. During the summer we had fed squirrels and birds; we had left peanuts and bread on the porch ledge. Climbing the porch steps, I smiled at the thought. Then something caught my eye – a bite-sized piece of piecrust stashed into the corner of the staircase, evidence of the 'crime'.

***

How many times have we been sorry for choosing to ignore our intuition – that persistent voice speaking from the soul, insistent on telling the truth? How many regretful experiences have we had because we disregarded our 'gut feeling'?

There is no tangible evidence to support or explain intuitive guidance. It is tempting to push a feeling away to focus on the noise in our head. We want to know the truth. But when Spirit provides it for us, we often question its origin. How can we accept an answer based entirely upon a feeling? How do we know that what we are feeling is truth, when there is nothing tangible upon which to base it?

Gut feelings are not logical or rational. They represent our inner knowing – the truth apart from fact or physical evidence. Intuition requires our total trust. It cannot be analyzed or rationalized, feared or doubted, judged or criticized. In fact, distrusting intuition signals Spirit to stop speaking.

Trusting the truth

Recognizing Spirit's voice isn't always easy. This experience taught me how to trust the truth.

It was three o'clock in the morning and I was alone in bed, struggling with my thoughts. My husband, John, had just started working the nightshift as a mail handler at the post office. This was his first night of training. According to the schedule, he should have been home hours before.

I rolled over and looked out my bedroom window into the basswood branches gently swaying in the summer wind. The up-and-down motion of the leaves soothed me. The sound of my own breath temporarily quieted the noise that was trying to build inside my brain.

I closed my eyes to pray. I attempted to visualize that my husband was all right. I tried to become peaceful, but I still felt anxious.

At five o'clock, I climbed out of bed and walked down the hall to look out the window. It was dark, but I was able to see the empty space in the driveway where my husband's car should have been. Trying to ignore my anxiety, I held onto trust as I made my way down the stairs. I was hoping to find him sleeping on the couch with the television on. My hopes were dashed as soon as I reached the living room. The TV was silent; the couch was empty.

Suddenly, 'What if' scenarios I had managed not to think about suddenly entered my mind. 'What if he hit a guardrail, the car flipped over and he landed upside-down in a ditch?' my mind conjured. 'What if someone was hiding behind the backseat of his car, jumped him, attacked him and left him alone to die? What if he suffered a heart attack while he was working and he's lying on a cold, hard floor? What if? What if? What if?' As my fear continued to intensify, so did the images I was creating in my head.

Another hour passed. John still hadn't come home. I could feel every muscle tighten in my anxiety. Holding onto trust and not allowing myself to succumb to panic was becoming an ever-increasing challenge.

Searching for a focus other than fear, I sat on the couch, opened the window and took some slow, deep breaths. The more slowly and deeply I breathed, the quieter I became. In the quiet, I realized I had a choice. Either I could continue to think fearful thoughts, allowing them to escalate into panic, or I could remain quiet and trust my intuition to guide me to my answers.

I sat still and continued to breathe slowly and deeply, concentrating on the rising and falling of my chest. As I exhaled fear and inhaled trust, each new breath began to fill me with calm and peace. The deeper I felt that energy, the more peaceful I became. Despite the direction in which panic was trying to take me, I chose to trust the peace and calm I was feeling in my heart.

It was seven o'clock in the morning. But in the quiet, without fear or negative thoughts to distract me, I was able to dismiss how late John was and trust he was OK. I closed my eyes to climb even more deeply into quiet when suddenly, out of nowhere, two words appeared in my head – *mandatory overtime*. Logically, they made no sense, but I knew not to question them.

Trusting my feelings over fear was challenging. I had no facts to support them. I had no tangible evidence that my husband was OK, just a whisper that had arisen from somewhere deep inside me – *mandatory overtime.*

At 7:15 a.m., exhausted from a sleepless night, I was determined to remain in a state of trust, even though fear was trying to find me. Every passing minute challenged me to remain strong and positive to silence the noise in my head. Some moments challenged me more than others.

At 7:31 a.m., I decided I had trusted enough. I grabbed the phone to dial a work number John had given me. It wasn't supposed to be active for another week, but it was all that I had. It took 20 or 30 rings to convince me that no one was there to answer my call.

When I put the phone down, I took some deep breaths. While I was breathing, I realized something. Deep down, I believed my husband was OK; I needed to trust what I was feeling in my heart. It was up to me to embrace my intuition.

The deepest calm overtook me in that moment of realization. Peace enveloped me, comforting and warming me all at once. Birds were singing in the trees; leaves were rustling in a rush of summer wind. The sky had changed from black to blue and the sun was shining.

For the next hour, I quietly focused on nature. The connectedness I felt to the world outside my window reminded me to be at peace within my soul.

Suddenly, a familiar sound interrupted my quiet – John's car pulling into the driveway. I ran outside to greet him and he rolled his window down to kiss me.

'I'm so happy you're home!' I said.

Before I could ask the question, he whispered my answer: 'Mandatory overtime'.

***

Intuition has guided me so many times. It was there the day I almost donated my eight-year-old son's baby clothes. For some inexplicable reason, I put them back in the attic where they had been stored. The next day, I discovered that I was pregnant with my second child.

It was there when I planned to run errands with my sister and changed my mind at the last minute. Shortly after she left, I heard sirens as police cars and an ambulance raced to the scene of her car crash. The passenger door of her vehicle was smashed into the steering wheel.

It was there the evening I answered a personal ad that led me to my husband…

As we become attuned to our intuition, we are able to recognize it when it surfaces. The more we recognize our inner voice, the more we are able to trust it. The more we trust it, the more guidance we receive as a reflection of that trust. As long as we are quiet and open-minded, we will feel our answers rising from our soul. As long as we trust and abide by our feelings, we are in alignment with our intuition.

Trusting Spirit's whisper can be challenging. Sometimes, it seems much easier to bypass the whisper from our heart to focus on the noise in our head. A whisper is soft; noise is loud. By its very nature, a soft voice is more difficult to hear than a loud one. But as we become quiet, not only are we able to recognize our intuition; we also know to trust it.

Like an echo sounding in the distance, Spirit's voice resonates from within our soul.

Chapter 2

Awareness

'It's not what you look at that matters; it's what you see.'
Henry David Thoreau

I was washing dishes one afternoon, occasionally gazing out the window to daydream. Winter's white blanket was wearing away to reveal green-brown edges. Birds were chirping. Squirrels were performing acrobatics in the trees. February was melting into March; winter was surrendering to spring.

This time of year made me think of my grandfather. It marked the anniversary of his passing. He had died many years before, while I was finishing my senior year in college. But at the moment, my focus was on the life he had shared with me.

Grandpa was alive and well in my mind. I pictured him concocting bran muffins in his kitchen. I saw him in the backyard of my childhood home, preparing the garden for pear tomatoes. I envisioned him as the gifted photographer he was, conducting photo sessions in his basement.

Memories played like a home movie in my head.

I remembered the tree house Grandpa built for my sisters and me, and the plastic kites he made for us. I recalled the day he taught us how to ride our bikes and the time he fashioned hats from newspaper to shield us from unexpected rain.

I held onto those memories as tightly as the dish I gripped in my hands. The more I focused on them, the more I sensed my grandfather's presence. It felt as though he was standing beside me. I spoke to him as if he was there.

I told him all the things I had felt but never expressed with words. I thanked him for letting me fish in the rain and teaching me not to leave the bait box in the sun. I thanked him for the wonderful stories he had shared with me, especially the funny ones. I thanked him for watching my sisters and me dance in the living room with scarves on our heads.

Then I stopped remembering, to watch the dogwood tree dancing in the wind. I stopped thinking to get quiet and just be.

In that moment of peace, I felt a tingling sensation throughout my body. I felt my grandfather's energy around me.

Whispering, 'I love you', I placed the last dish in the drying rack. I turned around to walk away, when something caught my attention. Prior to washing the dishes, I had swept and mopped the floor. Something small and shiny was directly in front of me – something I hadn't seen before.

For some reason, my focus shifted to the wall where my son's artwork was displayed. Although Valentine's Day had passed, Jp's homemade valentine was still hanging there. It was red with a white doily in the center. Surrounding the doily were red sequins. Now I noticed one of them was missing.

I bent down to pick up whatever was on the floor. My intention was to throw it away. For a moment, I hesitated; Spirit was asking me to take a second look. Placing the object into my palm, I held it under the light. Then the tiny heart-shaped sequin sent light back to me.

Postscript

I was editing this story. Grandpa would have said I was getting carried away, but there was a reason why. I wanted to convey every detail exactly as it had transpired. Desiring confirmation that my goal had been accomplished, I asked for his input.

Two hours later, my husband, John, returned home from grocery shopping. He was hiding something behind his back. I thought it was a bouquet of flowers. But when he placed his surprise in my hands, I started to cry.

My husband had given me an amazing thing: a beautiful

multi-colored kite. It was in perfect condition except for the missing string.

'Thank you,' I said, sobbing. 'Where did you buy this?' I asked.

'I didn't,' he said. 'I was driving through the park and saw it in a tree.'

'Durand?' I asked, knowing he often took drives there.

'No, I didn't find it at Durand,' he continued. 'It was at Cobbs Hill.'

My legs tingled – which is Spirit's way of capturing my attention. Cobbs Hill Park was where my sisters and I had learned how to fly kites. Grandpa was my teacher. My husband didn't know.

'He must have left this as a gift for you,' he said, when I told him.

The energy of truth surged through me again.

It was unseasonably warm and windy that day. In honor of my grandfather, I took my family to the park to fly the kite he had given me. Kneeling in the grass, I waited while John attached a new string. At the same time, I looked up at the sun. My mind was quiet. My body was still. My heart whispered, 'The sky is the limit!'

***

When we recognize spiritual messages in physical reality, we are 'spiritually aware'. Awareness enables us to identify, interpret and understand Spirit's efforts to communicate with us.

As we examine our physical world, what experiences are happening to us or near us? What is the universe trying to tell us?

Our answers lie in understanding that circumstances outside the soul reflect our current spiritual condition.

Remember, in order to experience awareness, we must be receptive to it. Therefore, anxiety, doubt and fear must be absent from our mind. A peaceful mind will attune us to Spirit's voice. It will enable us to understand what it is saying and why.

The following components must be in place in order for us to experience awareness.

The Desire to Know the Truth

Spirit is always speaking the truth to us. Our personal circumstances are directly related to what is happening within our soul. Our personal world is constantly mirroring a collective spiritual, emotional and physical state of being. In order to receive spiritual guidance, we must desire to know the deeper meanings of our physical circumstances. We must desire to know the truth.

Remember, our soul holds the answers to all the questions we could ever ask about ourselves. All we need to do to access them is ask for spiritual guidance. As long as we choose to be spiritually aware in our physical world, truth will find us.

Openness and Willingness to Receive Spiritual Guidance

We must be open and willing to accept spiritual guidance. Furthermore, we must be open as to how it manifests in physical form. For example, if we are confused about our career path and need to know if we are headed in the right direction, we may ask Spirit for confirmation. At the same time, we need to trust our answer to surface in a perfect way and at the perfect time.

Therefore, we would not specifically request that Spirit flicker the light across the street twice if our answer is 'Yes'. We would trust Spirit to answer our question without having to know how.

Trust that the Universe Will Guide Us to Our Answer

It is important to know that our question has an answer (or our problem has a solution). It is equally important to trust that our answer resides deep within us. The truth will surface in the best way and at the right time, to physically confirm what we spiritually know.

We must believe 'wholeheartedly' and without a doubt that we already know the answer. All we need to do is trust that answer to make itself known to us.

Readiness to Accept the Truth

Readiness pertains to our ability to accept the truth. If we trust the universe to provide us with our answer, we are in a state of readiness. However, if we ask for spiritual guidance while hoping for a particular outcome, or doubting or fearing the universe's response, we are not in the right frame of mind to accept the truth.

Synchronicity

When we are open, willing and ready to receive our answer, and we trust our answer to find us, the universe will provide it for us.

Synchronicity is a 'divinely timed coincidence' orchestrated by the universe. It happens when we are in the right place at the right time to receive spiritual guidance. Its function is to allow us to know the truth.

***

The following stories depict what spiritual awareness looks like in real life.

I was 35 years old when I learned how to drive. Although I had attended driving school and passed my road test, I doubted my driving capabilities. Even unsolicited reassurance from family and friends failed to instill confidence in me. I needed confirmation that I was a good driver.

Knowing the universe would provide it for me, I quieted my mind. With closed eyes, breathing slowly and deeply, I prayed. Trusting my answer to find me, I silently asked my question: 'Am I qualified to drive?'

The next morning, I was driving down a familiar road when suddenly a pedestrian darted out in front of me. I quickly swerved to avoid hitting him. Minutes later, an oncoming car crossed the center line into my lane, forcing me to steer the car out of harm's way. Shortly afterward, the car in front of me stopped abruptly at a green light, causing me to slam on my brakes.

Fortunately, I remained calm and in control of my vehicle during every challenge Spirit had arranged for me. I passed my tests. There was just one problem. I still doubted my driving skills.

A few days later, I was driving my son home from T-Ball. Without warning, the car to my left tried to veer into my lane. There wasn't enough room for him. I was too close to the car ahead of me.

The light changed. We were stopped at an intersection. The driver was shouting, but his words were unintelligible. I had no difficulty understanding him, however, when he leaped over his seat to the passenger side, opened the door, walked to my car and screamed, 'Do you know how to drive?!'

Although he was upset, I knew that I had done nothing wrong.

When the light turned green I started driving again. The motion of the car soothed me and quieted my mind. In my state of being, I realized something: a stranger had asked me the question I had posed to the universe. Another moment of silence led me to my answer: I am qualified to drive. I needed to trust myself.

***

Katie and I had been friends for years. We called each other every day, often more than once. We had dinner together whenever we could. We made each other laugh and cry. Katie and I were close

– more like sisters than friends. She was a blessing to me.

But as time passed, my life changed. Motherhood led me in a different direction. Suddenly, there were soccer games and karate classes to attend. There was homework to help with; there were play dates to arrange. My days overflowed with new things to do and places to go. There was little time left for anything else.

The busier our lives became, the less room there was for each other.

Once in a while we were able to connect. Unfortunately, we were no longer making good use of our time. Instead of celebrating being together, we were complaining about how difficult our lives had become. To make matters worse, negativity was turning our conversations into arguments; neither of us could hear what the other was saying.

It was during a phone call with Katie when I realized Spirit was trying to tell me something. For the first few minutes of our conversation, everything was fine. But as soon as I started expressing my opinion, the phone acted up.

First, static muffled our words. Then our connection broke, preventing whoever was speaking at the time from being heard by the other. At one point, we were completely disconnected. The phone went dead.

It happened in the middle of a heated argument. Katie thought I had hung up on her; I thought she had hung up on me.

While I wanted to logically justify our poor connection, my heart knew better. I heard the universe. I received the message it had sent me. I didn't want to believe it, although deep down I knew I had no choice. Katie and I were disconnecting from each other, and Spirit was speaking the truth.

Confused and broken-hearted, I decided a drive would clear my head. On the way to the car, I held the key chain Katie had given me. Its inscription read, '... And I shall guard and protect you in all your ways'. Not only was that quote a reminder that my angel was watching over me; it was also a message from Katie that she would always be there for me.

As soon as I turned my key in the lock, I heard a snap followed by a jingling sound. My key chain had broken away from my key, landing in the driveway, angel-side down.

A film of tears blurred my vision as I picked it up from the pavement. I understood the messages Spirit had been sending me – powerful depictions of the word 'disconnection'. There was no mistaking this one.

It didn't surprise me when, shortly afterward, a misunderstanding caused Katie and me to take a break from our friendship. Years later, we tried to reconnect, but it was clear to me that life was continuing to lead us in opposite directions. Trusting the truth I felt in my heart, I made the painful decision to let Katie go. Sadly, we have been separated ever since.

***

I was reading my pregnancy book, preparing for my first child's birth. My due date was fast approaching; I was starting to feel nervous. Leafing through pages, I looked for something to ease my mind.

Suddenly, my book slipped out of my hands and fell to the floor.

Leaving it in its exact position, I picked it up and placed it in my lap. When I turned the book over, I noticed something. It had opened to the first page of the 'Emergency Caesarean' chapter.

The universe had my attention. I had never read that part of the book. The subject was so frightening to me that I deliberately skipped over it. My prenatal class had also addressed the topic; I made sure I was absent that day.

Now I was looking at something I didn't even want to think about. Heightening my anxiety was the awareness that my thumb was pointing to a paragraph regarding umbilical cord entanglement.

A cold chill ran down my legs, commanding my attention. Recognizing Spirit's attempt to reach me, I forced myself to read every word of the chapter I had avoided.

Twenty-three hours later, I went into labor. Nineteen hours after that, I was ready to give birth. But things weren't progressing as I had anticipated. John and I watched the fetal monitor, hoping to discover why.

Each time I had a contraction, the baby's heart rate fell slightly. As the contractions increased in intensity and duration, the numbers on the screen dropped even more. At one point, all we saw was a red blur where the numbers had been. Our baby's heart rate had plummeted into the danger zone. He was in fetal distress.

Before I realized what was happening, doctors and nurses had taken over the room. The anesthesiologist was giving me morphine, a nurse was fitting me with a catheter, and another nurse was placing an oxygen mask over my face. As I was being wheeled to the operating room for an emergency C-section, a different nurse held half her hand inside me to prevent the umbilical cord from being compressed.

Minutes later, my healthy son, John Paul, made his entrance into the world. My obstetrician explained what had complicated his birth – he had become entangled in his umbilical cord.

***

My five-year-old son, John Paul (Jp), was receiving speech therapy three times a week. This required him to be transported from his school to another location. Even though I was assured he would be supervised going to and from class, I had doubts.

Since school was close to home, I usually walked there to pick him up at dismissal time. One day when I wasn't feeling well, I asked my neighbor, Erin, for a ride.

Erin always left her house early to pick up her son, who

attended the same class as mine. The parking lot filled up quickly. She wanted to make sure she found a space. I made a point to leave at the last minute. Parking wasn't a consideration.

That day, we left for school 20 minutes earlier than I would have, had I walked. Ironically, backed-up traffic detained us from reaching our destination. At one point, we were stopped directly across from the front entrance. For some reason, I glanced in that direction.

On the front steps there was a little boy who had been left outside alone. He was jumping up and down, struggling to reach the intercom. The button he needed to press was two feet over his head.

As I focused on him, I became aware of details I might otherwise have missed. His book bag looked familiar. I recognized his jacket. I knew this little boy – he was my son!

I got out of the car and ran to Jp. Holding him in my arms, I kissed his tear-stained face. Pressing the intercom button, I alerted the office to open the door. When I reported the incident to the principal, she assigned an escort to my son, promising that such a thing would never happen again. Fortunately, it never did.

Had I walked to school that day, I would never have known that Jp was standing outside alone. I would not have seen him because I would have walked to the parking lot behind the building to pick him up. Furthermore, due to his articulation delay, he would not have been able to tell me what had happened. My son would have been upset and I would not have known why.

Thankfully, Spirit placed me in the right place at the right time.

***

I had mixed feelings. My husband and I were ready to make a

purchase offer on a house. It was beautiful. There were five bedrooms, two and a half baths, a fireplace, balcony, hardwood floors and a sizeable backyard. On the flipside, it was located on a busy city street in a high crime area. It was also a foreclosure property, which made me feel uncomfortable.

I had a difficult decision to make. A family had just lost their home. How could I feel good about benefiting from their misfortune? On the other hand, we had never found anything that matched our expectations until now. Confused, I pushed my feelings aside to keep the facts in mind. Then I scheduled an appointment with our realtor.

Our meeting took place outdoors at a neighborhood coffee shop, on a sunny spring day. Our objective was to put a bid on the house and sign any necessary paperwork. Everything was going smoothly until our realtor handed us the contract.

John was getting ready to sign it when, out of nowhere, a stiff breeze lifted it from his hands. Thinking nothing of it, he retrieved the paper from the lawn. As soon as he tried to pen his signature again, the same thing happened. His third attempt to sign his name was equally unsuccessful. At one point he looked at me and said, 'Do you think this is a bad omen?' The realtor, afraid to hear my answer, suggested that we sign the papers indoors.

The next day, we learned our offer had been accepted. We went away for the weekend to celebrate.

The following morning, our realtor called again. This time the news wasn't good. Apparently, there had been a misunderstanding. We had lost the house to another couple that had outbid us. They had been in the picture the entire time.

Our house had been removed from our hands. Then again, it had never been ours in the first place.

***

The universe provides us with the guidance we need, exactly when we need it. Spirit places us in the right situation at the right time. Awareness and insight afford us the opportunity to understand why, and trust enables us to receive and believe our message.

As I write this chapter titled 'Awareness', amazing examples of awareness are finding me. The following story demonstrates Spirit's limitless potential to capture our attention.

Nicole comforted her partner, Jacob, as his spirit prepared to depart from his body. Jacob had cancer. Doctors had told him his condition was terminal. Yet Jacob fought to remain in the only world he had known while Nicole lovingly guided him toward transformation.

Cancer was taking its toll. Painfully thin and drained of energy, Jacob's body was little more than a shell. Even so, Nicole looked beyond the man she saw, to comfort the soul she knew. More than anything else, Jacob longed for peace in his incomprehensible world and Nicole was determined to bring it to him.

One morning, she became aware of an opportunity. Jacob's pajamas were old and worn. They hung from his overly slight frame. Knowing he would appreciate wearing something soft and elegant, Nicole offered to buy him new ones. Jacob liked the idea and supplied her with specifications.

Without delay, Nicole launched her search. The task, however, soon proved to be challenging. Nowhere did she see the gold silk pajamas Jacob had requested, nor could she find anything in his size. Although her efforts had left her empty-handed and exhausted, she decided to make one last stop.

After scanning another sleepwear department without success, Nicole was prepared to admit defeat. It was then, however, that a beautiful pair of pajamas attracted her attention. They were gold, made of silk and the right size – exactly what Jacob had requested. Without thinking twice, Nicole purchased the pajamas and brought them home to him.

Jacob was delighted. He couldn't wait to slip into his new pajamas. Nicole helped him get dressed and told him how regal he looked in gold silk. As she smoothed out the fabric, Nicole noticed the label peeking out of the neckline. Since she had purchased the pajamas without knowing their designer, she read the name before tucking it back inside.

For a moment Nicole forgot to breathe. Tears ran down her face. Chills raced up her spine. But she kept what she saw to herself.

Two days passed. Nicole waited at Jacob's bedside as he drew his last breaths. His spirit departed peacefully, as she held him in her arms. Jacob's earthly work was done. His soul's mission had been accomplished. The time had come for her to say 'Goodbye'.

Kissing his forehead, Nicole whispered sweet words to her love. They were the same words that were imprinted upon the label of his pajamas –'Jacob Goodnight'.

***

We turn on the radio and hear song lyrics speaking words of wisdom in the exact moment we need to hear them. We are in the library seeking guidance on a particular topic and the perfect book suddenly falls off a shelf and lands at our feet. We are dining at a restaurant, wondering how to realize our life's dream, when we overhear a conversation that guides us in the right direction.

Through awareness, we recognize and understand the spiritual truths of our physical circumstances. We realize that our answers always find us at the perfect time and in a perfect way.

Chapter 3

Signs and Symbols

Knowingly or unknowingly, we are sending messages out into the universe. Thoughts we think, words we speak and actions we take translate collectively into a statement from which we create our reality. Just as we are 'messaging' Spirit, indicating the direction we are taking in our life, so Spirit is returning the favor.

I had just typed the paragraph above and was attempting to save it in my computer. In the process, my finger hit a key I had never used before. As a result the screen went black. Then unfamiliar words appeared across it: 'Initialize? Yes or No?' Having never seen the question, I didn't know its meaning. However, I knew one thing – looking at it was making me more than uncomfortable.

Never had I experienced a gut feeling as visceral as this one. Anxiety gripped my stomach, twisting it into knots. My pulse raced; my throat became parched. My head throbbed with panic, making it difficult to think. Had one paragraph disappeared, my reaction would have been less dramatic. Under the circumstances, it was warranted. More than 20 pages of work were in jeopardy.

Despite all signs pointing in a negative direction, I tried my best to fix my 'mistake'. First, I employed the logical approach – entering the 'Cancel' command to correct my error. Unfortunately, either my logic was faulty or my machine was being uncooperative. The only thing that maneuver accomplished was to change the screen from black to blue.

My second idea was born from common sense. Answering the question seemed like a straightforward solution. But when I played it safe by choosing 'No', nothing happened. Even repeatedly pounding on the return key as if to emphatically answer 'No!' was met by no response. The only thing I achieved, aside from relieving my frustration, was to freeze the question I had been trying to delete.

The next option was my last resort: answering 'Yes' to the question I didn't understand. Although I was uncomfortable about using this tactic, nothing else had worked. I was becoming impatient.

Reluctantly I made my selection, hoping I was doing the right thing. The screen flashed again; I thought my effort was successful. Seconds later, I discovered I was only half right. The good news was that I had erased the words I didn't understand. The bad news was that I had also cleared away the chapter I had hoped to save. Apparently, 'Initialize?' meant 'Would you like to write this entire chapter, word for word, over again from memory?'

I would like to report that spiritual openness and awareness peacefully and immediately guided me to answers. But staring at a blank screen that had been filled with detailed spiritual insights left me in a place just short of hysteria. I was devastated; all I could do was search my mind for an explanation. In all the noise, however, my answer was inaudible. Disheartened by what had happened without understanding why, I temporarily abandoned my manuscript. I thought the universe had told me to stop writing it.

It took some time for me to calm down, reconnect with Spirit and resume writing this book – months in fact. When I finally quieted my mind, I accepted that my chapter had been lost for a reason, trusting that one day I would understand why.

Rewriting those words was not something I was eager to do. But I began to relax the moment I realized something: what was lost in my computer was stored within my soul. To access my words, all I needed to do was to trust that I knew them.

I stilled my mind to allow the chapter I had once written to resurface. Eventually, when it did, I typed it entirely from memory.

One day, what had happened to me and why became clear. I realized that I had been sending a message to the universe. Privately and silently inside my head, I had been repeatedly asking a question: 'Anyone can write this book – why me?' Additionally, I was speaking those words to family and friends.

Without any awareness, I had engaged Spirit in conversation.

As painful as my lesson had been, it had happened for a reason. Rewriting this chapter reminded me of why I was writing this book. I had learned how to see life through Spirit's eyes. I needed to share my stories, so others could do the same.

***

Spirit is always speaking to us. Sometimes it offers a quiet suggestion. Sometimes it raises its voice to attract our attention. When we recognize Divine Guidance, regardless of its form, we strengthen our ever-present connection with the universe.

Knowing Spirit's voice is important. Even more significant is being able to understand the message it is trying to convey. At times, however, translating the language of the universe may seem challenging. But if we remember that Spirit knows our answer, and trust it to surface at the perfect time and in a perfect way, understanding our message can be effortless.

The language of the universe is uncomplicated. Spirit speaks clearly and powerfully in order to deliver our message. If we are quiet we can hear the whisper. We know when the universe is trying to tell us something. It brings us to wherever we need to be, whenever we need to be there. Then, once we are in position, it shines a light on our truths to make us aware of them.

From the vantage point of Spirit, we see the significance beyond the surface of 'what is'. In the light of truth, everything has meaning. When the car breaks down, it means something.

When we lose our wallet, it means something. When the sink gets clogged, it means something. The question remains – what does it mean?

One might argue that cars stop working, wallets get lost and sinks get clogged – all for a reason. But what if something more significant is taking place, beyond what we see? What if the universe is trying to tell us something?

Our world is filled with signs and symbols that are universally recognized and understood. They tell us when to stop, when to go and when to exhibit caution. They direct us around detours and warn us of potential challenges and dangers. We pay attention to traffic signals and road signs because we know they hold meaning and purpose. We use maps to guide us to our destinations because we trust them to help us find our way to wherever we are going. We take signs and symbols seriously because we are taught that not doing so could cause serious repercussions.

Spirit has its own version of signs and symbols. Like traffic signals, road signs and maps, these devices remind us to remain alert, watch our speed and beware of changing road conditions. There is one difference, though. The meanings they hold are divine.

At first glance, spiritual signs and symbols are ordinary things, and from a physical perspective we accept them at face value. A bird is a bird, a flower is a flower, and a penny is a penny. But the universe sees things differently. From a spiritual standpoint, life holds metaphorical meaning. A bird could symbolize freedom, a flower might represent a blossoming spirit, and a penny could signify good fortune. Divine light transforms everyday things into extraordinary messages. In order to recognize them, all we need to do is be open to seeing life in a different way.

Here is a story that shows how anything can be spiritually significant. It all depends on how we look at it.

Sitting down to repair my sweater, I wondered if I should try. It was 20 years old. There were so many holes in it. A chill traveled through me as I picked up dropped stitches; my mind revisited the past.

Knitting had always been one of my passions. The process fascinated me. There was something magical about it. As a child I watched my mother transform yarn into works of art. One day, she handed me her knitting needles and showed me what to do. Ever since then, my enthusiasm for the craft has never waned.

Even after I had graduated from college, I was knitting. While I was living with my parents, it became a nightly ritual.

One evening, my mother and I were looking at her yarn collection. Each skein was as exquisite as the next. She had an idea. There was more than enough yarn for two sweaters. We could use a simple pattern as a stitch guide and come up with our own designs.

I couldn't wait to get started.

Reaching into the basket, I selected my materials. Excited about my project, I grabbed my knitting needles and sat on the floor. I tried to think of an idea, but nothing was happening. The more I tried to think of something, the more inspiration eluded me.

Tired of waiting, I grabbed some black yarn and started knitting. By the time I had finished the waistband, my mind had quieted down. I had started to make a red stripe and suddenly changed my mind. For no apparent reason and in the middle of a row, I changed colors again. From then on, I decided to switch colors whenever I felt like it. Without thinking, I would trade one yarn for another. It would be an experiment. Instead of me designing my sweater, my sweater would design itself.

The more I knitted, the more peaceful I became. After some time had passed, I peeked at my work. An interesting design had started to form on its own. Distinct black shapes stood out against a red background. One of them looked like a 'thunderbird'.

I stared at it for the longest time. I couldn't draw a picture of a thunderbird, let alone knit one.

As I kept knitting, more pictures appeared. Thinking I had channeled a past-life memory, I gave my sweater a name. The red background reminded me of the sky just before dusk. The black shapes looked like a configuration of rectangular stones. I called my sweater 'Stonehenge at Sunset'.

When I finished knitting the back, I started working on the front. A picture appeared this time as well. It was a continuation of the design I had created. I had knitted another 'thunderbird'. This time it was blue. My mother handed me a red bead; she thought it should have an eye.

As I mended my sweater, my mind traveled back through time. I remembered the circumstances of my life 20 years before. I didn't know who I was or where I was going.

Using whatever yarn I had in my basket, I knitted new material to fill the holes. I sewed old yarns and new yarns together to close them. In my meditative state, I was inspired to be creative. I crocheted a red edge around the black neckline. Embroidery mended the smaller holes while adding an artistic flourish.

Holding my sweater in my hands, I remembered the times I almost let it go. I had tried to donate it; John took it out of the box. There had been a flood in the basement; I found it underwater. Thinking it was ruined, I threw it away. My husband rescued it again.

Every time I tried to let go of my sweater, it came back to me. Until recently, I never understood why.

While I was writing this story, my six-year-old son, Thomas, placed the sweater on the floor to look at it. The pictures intrigued him. Immediately, he identified every image he saw. Thomas described the back of the sweater first. He named all the black shapes. There was a body of water. A bridge was over it. A bird was 'flying' above. Black clouds were over its head. Above them was a road – a place to walk.

His words sent shivers throughout my body. The pictures he had described were symbolic of my spiritual journey. Every image was a metaphor. The bridge symbolized the transition I would be making – leaving my parents' home to start a new life. The black clouds represented fear and depression – challenges I faced on the way to truth. The road was symbolic of the spiritual path I would take.

The thunderbird was 'Spirit'.

Thomas turned the sweater over. In that quiet moment, I saw things I had never been aware of before. There was an enormous house above the blue thunderbird. It had many windows and doors. A hole I had repaired looked like a person standing in a doorway.

I was looking at a depiction of my present-day life. My Higher Self had guided me home.

Spirit had designed a timeless message; now, I understand the meaning behind the pictures. I hold the power to take myself wherever I desire to go. It is within me. It is within us all.

***

What Does This Mean?

Signs and symbols are to Spirit what words are to our physical self. They are a means of expression, a mode of communication, a messenger and a message – instruments through which information is conveyed and relayed. What constitutes a sign or symbol? Anything the universe uses as an attention-getting device such as shattered glass, a broken garbage disposal, a five-dollar bill in the street, a dime heads-up on a sidewalk... Making the distinction between a common incident, event or occurrence, and something derived from the Divine, is a matter of perception. The way in which we perceive something determines not only what we see, but also how we see it. From a physical stance, we see only its surface, but from a spiritual perspective we see into the heart of our situation, where a deeper truth resides.

It must also be stated that in order for our message to be spiritually significant, we must recognize it as such. A sign or symbol, no matter how powerful, is meaningless unless it means something to us.

Spirit is always telling us the truth. But as this story illustrates, we are not always ready to listen.

My oldest son and I had almost finished decorating our Christmas tree. Glowing strings of lights illuminated every branch. Red velvet bows accented its rounded-triangular shape. All we needed to do was hang a few more ornaments to cover the bare spots and our project would be complete.

After placing the remaining decorations, we intended to view the tree from a distance. However, we were unable to follow through with our plan. As soon as we turned around, the tree fell on top of us.

My back and shoulders carried its weight, while sharp pine needles dug into my skin through my clothes. At the same time, panic surged through me. Beneath heavy branches, lights and smashed ornaments was my six-year-old son, Jp, and in my position, I couldn't help him. Fortunately, I was able to raise my back high enough, so he could crawl out to a clean, dry floor. Then shortly afterward I followed him.

I hugged my little boy, hoping he couldn't feel my racing heart. My mind was spinning; I needed to slow it down. I picked up the splintered glass and pine needles that had been scattered across the room. While I was mopping the floor, a question arose from my soul.

What did it mean? I had no clue and would have to wait to

find out.

My husband had returned home and was studying the scene in front of him. He asked for an explanation, so I told him what had happened. Then we lifted the tree and set it into its stand, hoping it would remain there.

My soul asked me to be quiet. My mind wouldn't stay still. I wanted to know the real reason why that tree had fallen. But I wasn't ready to learn what it was. 'Logical me' needed to cite the homemade tree stand as the cause. 'Spiritual me' knew the truth. What had happened was more than a matter of physics. Spirit had sent me a sign.

The next morning, I reached into half-empty boxes, hoping to find enough ornaments to redecorate our tree. At the same time, my brain sought logic to explain the previous day's event. By the time I had finished hanging bows, lights and decorations, I was almost convinced the tree had fallen for purely physical reasons. Then an ornament fell to the floor, followed by the tree, which again landed on top of me.

There wasn't time to panic. It had come down so fast and with such force that it pinned me to the floor. Thankfully, my son wasn't with me. Fortunately, I remembered how to escape from such a predicament. Closing my eyes to avoid scratching them, I lifted my back and crawled away.

My circumstances felt staged and surreal like a scene from a contrived, predictable Christmas comedy. But I wasn't laughing.

Like a child who had been scolded without good reason, I wanted to know why the universe had raised its voice.

Unfortunately, the quiet I needed in order to hear Spirit eluded me; my mind was filled with noise. Hoping to understand my situation, I invited the universe to play a game of charades.

'Should I beware of falling trees?' I silently asked, anxiously awaiting a response. When there was none, I reached into the dark for deeper meaning. 'Is something bad about to befall me?'

I wondered as I began to panic. My second question went unanswered as well. Having yet to receive a reply, my thoughts ventured in a different direction. Maybe Spirit was saying, *Robin, you're Jewish. You're not allowed to celebrate Christmas.*

The more I analyzed my situation, the more my answers escaped me. I had dissected my sign into so many pieces that I didn't know what I was looking at anymore. Furthermore, my head was throbbing from trying to figure it out.

I needed to rest, but there was too much to do. In addition to mothering and providing entertainment for my son, I had clients to counsel, letters to write, cards to send and pumpkin breads to bake. When those responsibilities had been fulfilled, there was shopping to do and errands to run.

My life was out of control. But not until I had tried to re-warm my coffee in the laundry shoot was I ready to admit it. Having neither the desire nor time to change my ways, I continued conducting life on 'fast forward'. Spirit had no other alternative than to contact me again.

This time it happened while I was setting the toaster oven timer. Ordinarily it would make a ticking sound, but on this occasion I heard nothing when I turned the dial. The timer had worked that morning to make toast. 'Why isn't it working now?' I wondered.

I had barely finished my thought when a high-pitched alarm interrupted my concentration. It was the stove timer. I had used it the day before while I was baking cookies but hadn't used it since. Now the oven was empty. There was no need for it to be on. It was ringing to the depths of me; I needed to shut it off. There was just one problem. When I tried to turn the dial, it wouldn't budge.

In all the years I had used the timer it had never jammed. Now, it was frozen in place. I couldn't pull it out, I couldn't push it in and it wouldn't turn in any direction. I tried almost everything I could think of to make the dial move, but nothing worked.

Finally, in desperation, I grabbed a pair of pliers, clamped down as hard as I could and shut the timer off by force.

I felt as though someone was screaming at me in a foreign language through a megaphone. Although Spirit's voice was unmistakable, I couldn't understand it. All I needed to do was get quiet to find out. Instead, and again, I tried analyzing my way to answers.

What were the chances, I asked myself, that two timers would break at the same time on the same day? Had my time come? Had time run out? Was this the end of time? And how did two timers breaking at the same time on the same day relate to a Christmas tree that had fallen on me twice?

I had no answers, only questions, as I analyzed the signs and symbols Spirit had given me. None of the conclusions I had drawn, according to what had been happening to me, made sense. Frustrated and mentally exhausted, I was incapable of thinking another thought. There was only one thing I could do in my state of mind.

It was late afternoon – Oprah was on. I sat down to watch my favorite show, but something was wrong with the TV. When I pressed the power button, there was sound but no picture. Tired and annoyed at having to fix another broken thing, I waited patiently for a picture to materialize on its own.

About five minutes later, my patience had run out and the picture hadn't returned. I needed to do something. Pretending that I understood the problem and how to correct it, I walked over to the TV to manipulate every button, switch and knob. Other than darkening the screen even more, my efforts accomplished nothing. Having exhausted almost every resource, there was only one more tactic to try.

'Something's wrong with the TV!' I yelled up the stairs, hoping my husband would hear me. 'I'm getting sound, but no picture!' I continued without receiving a reply. 'Did you hear me?!' I screamed more loudly. 'I said: I'm not getting the picture!'

Still, there was no response.

I paused to get quiet. There was no point trying to communicate with someone who couldn't hear me. I sank into my favorite chair to close my eyes and rest. As I began to fall asleep, the last words I had spoken echoed in my stillness. 'I'm not getting the picture.'

An hour later, I awoke from my nap. Everything on me and in me ached or was hot. I couldn't move my heavy, dizzy head and if I tried, nausea gripped me while the room spun. Every cell of me was screaming, 'I'm exhausted! Please take care of me!' Finally, I was in position, not only to hear, but also to listen to what Spirit had to say.

I sat in my chair with my eyes closed – not thinking, not doing, just being. As ill as I was, it felt good to be still. My world had come to a stop; my mind was quiet. I was ready to piece together my puzzle of signs and symbols.

Suddenly, Spirit's messages made sense. Like the unbalanced Christmas tree that held too many ornaments, I had become unbalanced from carrying too many responsibilities. Like the broken timers, I too had lost track of time.

I needed to take care of myself. I needed to make time for myself.

Finally, I got the picture.

***

Determining the meaning of our message can be challenging. We study every detail, hoping to discover its symbolic significance. But is every detail important when it comes to translating 'spirit speak'? When we break down our message into components through analysis, we lose the meaning of the whole among its parts. In other words, we have taken apart the 'big picture', leaving meaningless details in its place.

But finding spiritual meaning in our physical circumstances

can be effortless, if we go about it correctly. All we need to do is interpret our message.

Interpretation and analysis are not the same thing. When we interpret something, we are looking at the whole of it while asking, 'What does this mean?' Analysis, on the other hand, assigns individual meaning to the parts belonging to the whole.

Therefore, if interpretation is putting a puzzle together, analysis is taking that puzzle apart.

Through interpretation, Spirit will guide us to our answer. All we need to do is focus on the meaning of the big picture. For example, an eagle is flying overhead. We want to understand its spiritual implications, so we concentrate on the entire incident. It doesn't matter what color eyes it has, how big its wings are or how many clouds are in the sky. What is important is the meaning of the picture in its entirety and how we can personally relate to it.

It must be noted, however, that if we find ourselves focusing on a striking detail of our situation, Spirit has showcased it for us to see. For instance, the eagle is injured in some way or is flying through fog to reach its destination. In either case, we need to incorporate that specific detail into our interpretation. How will we know the significant details from the insignificant ones? Spirit will shine light on the things we are meant to notice.

The following guideline will help us interpret and understand our message:

Describe the situation
How does the situation relate to my life?

Describe the Situation

In a quiet frame of mind, without thinking or analyzing, describe what you see. You may accomplish this quietly in your mind, write down the description or say the words out loud. You may even choose to depict the situation artistically through painting, drawing, etc. Use whatever method is most effective for you.

Trust Spirit to provide you with the words (or artwork) that are symbolically meaningful for your circumstances. They will be the first words or images that come to mind.

For instance, an eagle is flying freely through the sky.

How does This Situation Relate to My Life?

Again, in a quiet frame of mind, without thinking or analyzing what you see, trust that you know your answer and allow it to surface. It may happen immediately or it may take some time to learn the truth. Let go of needing to know the answer in that moment. Know that it will surface when you are most receptive and be open to how it is delivered.

For instance, when I look at the eagle flying freely, I feel free as if I can take myself anywhere.

In this case, Spirit would be speaking to whatever has happened (is happening or about to happen) in our life to 'set us free'. Maybe we are beginning our life's work, or ending an abusive relationship, or going off to college for the first time. Remember, whatever our answer is, Spirit knows it and will shine light wherever it needs to, when we are ready to see the truth.

The following are examples of signs and symbols as they occurred in my life and how I determined their meanings through interpretation.

Example 1

Describe the situation: I had just finished speaking with an emotional client and went to the basement to check on my laundry. I noticed the dryer hose had become disconnected from the dryer.

How does this situation relate to my life? It is symbolic of disconnection. It is a reminder for me to emotionally disconnect from my work.

Example 2

Describe the situation: For some reason, my car wouldn't start, nor would my husband's. I needed to run some errands, but couldn't leave my home.

How does this situation relate to my life? It is symbolic of stillness. Rather than focusing on all the things I needed to do, I needed to stay home and be still.

Understanding our message is not equivalent to applying it to our circumstances. Just because we 'get it' doesn't mean we will use it to improve the quality of our life. Often, the universe will deliver the same message repeatedly, increasing its intensity with each new sign or symbol it employs until we have taken it 'to heart'.

What happens when Spirit sends us something too complicated for us to understand? Or what if, despite our best intentions to interpret our message, we end up analyzing it instead?

In the event that we are overcome with frustration (or any other energy in opposition to truth), our answer cannot make itself known to us in all our noise. This is the time to let go of any negative energy that would prevent spiritual insights from reaching us, including anxiety, fear, judgment and anger. When we have made room for our answer – when we are quiet, open and aware – we have indicated to Spirit that we trust it to find us.

The universe will continue sending us the same message, using whatever means are available to reach us. Only when we have successfully received, accurately interpreted and fully understood its spiritual implications, will Spirit stop sending it.

When there are no more signs or symbols to interpret, Spirit is telling us, *The subject has been closed.*

Sometimes we can determine the meaning of a sign or symbol

immediately. We become quiet to connect with our intuition, giving it permission to guide us to our answer. Other times, our head is heavy with noise, making it impossible to hear our heart speaking the truth.

Remember, Spirit knows our answer. Without thinking and without trying to figure things out, we must trust our intuition to guide us to it. If we are thinking, we are not intuiting. If we are analyzing our message (taking our sign or symbol apart), we are not interpreting (putting our puzzle pieces together). When we are ready and willing to know the truth, it will find us, at the perfect time and in a perfect way.

However, if we seek our answers in the midst of anxiety, exhaustion, frustration, panic or any state representing disconnection from our source, not only will we lead ourselves to more questions, but we will also lead ourselves away from our answer – serving only to intensify that negative emotion we are feeling.

Whether Spirit speaks softly, or in its loudest voice, its reasons for doing so are the same – to make us aware of where we are standing on life's path, to guide us ever forward into our Highest Good.

As we begin to embrace spiritual meaning in our physical world, we will be able to hear Spirit's whisper everywhere. But we must be patient because learning a new language takes time.

Be quiet. Be aware. Be open and willing to receive messages from the universe. Spirit will whisper their meanings to us. Whenever it becomes too noisy to hear, be still. Spirit will reach us wherever we are.

***

Ever since I can remember, I have looked to Spirit for guidance. Signs and symbols have provided direction for me so many times. They have prepared me for life's next adventure. They have soothed and comforted me during my most challenging moments, reminding me to trust and be who I am.

Most recently, Spirit arranged three reminders for me to slow down. First, a policeman pulled me over to issue a verbal warning. Second, I was forced to follow a car at 25 m.p.h for 20 minutes without being able to pass it. Third, when I refused to respond to the first two messages, I ended up causing a crash. At a red light, with both my sons in the car, I slammed on the accelerator instead of the brake and went into the car in front of us. Fortunately, no one in either car was injured.

***

Signs and symbols are wherever we are, whether we are looking straight ahead, left or right, up or down, or over our shoulder. They are mirrors placed on our path in order for our invisible Spirit to see its reflection.

Sometimes Spirit whispers to us. Sometimes it taps us on the shoulder. Then there are times when it hits us over the head with a message, until its meaning sinks into our soul. When we redefine our world according to Spirit, life takes on new meaning. Not only can we see better in the light, but we can also see the truth.

Chapter 4

Dreams

I can't believe this is happening. It's the first day of school and I've lost my schedule. It's not on my desk, in my purse, on top of my dresser, or anywhere in this dorm room. I don't know what to do. Class is about to start, but I can't remember where it is or what subject I'm studying. Who is my teacher? Why don't I have any supplies? Where are my clothes? Why am I here?

Signs and symbols not only accompany us while we're awake, but they also follow us into our dreams. Just because our body is sleeping doesn't mean Spirit is at rest. Dreams deliver messages to us when, freed from life's distractions, we are quiet enough to receive them.

Here is a story that gives meaning to those words.

I know the scenario above intimately and refer to it by name: 'The School Dream'. During the past 20 years, it has haunted me in various settings and under numerous circumstances. It has taken place in grade school, high school and college. It has centered on taking tests for which I am completely unprepared, giving presentations on subjects that are foreign to me, and wandering around campuses, hoping to find my teachers and classrooms by chance. As consistent as its theme has been, I have never had the same dream twice. The only thing that repeats itself is the storyline: school is starting and I have no schedule.

'The School Dream' is unsettling. It transports me to a time when anxiety and fear filled me instead of self-confidence. It brings me to a place where I cringed whenever a teacher called my name. It forces me to relive the moment I had to solve an algebra problem in front of the class, when my pounding heart obliterated every formula I had memorized.

Although I have been experiencing this dream for most of my adult life, my reason for having it remained a mystery.

It was during a conversation with a friend that my answer revealed itself. Cheryl and I were discussing 'The School Dream'. I wanted to know why I was still having it. I wanted to learn its meaning. After supplying her with the details of my most recent one, I listened while she offered her insights.

Immediately, she zeroed in on something I hadn't considered before: my clothes weren't in the dorm room. Then she told me why. 'You don't live there,' she said.

Cheryl's interpretation made sense and suddenly so did my dream. No wonder I had no school supplies. No wonder I didn't know my teacher's name or where my classroom was located. No wonder I couldn't remember what course I was taking – I wasn't supposed to be there! Before I could reiterate my revelations, she insightfully closed our conversation. 'You don't need to learn the lesson,' she said. 'Someone else does.'

I reached for my notebook to make notes for this chapter but picked up my dream journal instead. Having forgotten my earlier entry, I reread it. It was the last thing I had said before my dream ended: 'I don't go to school here. I graduated a long time ago.'

***

Dreams are dramas – private movies in our mind that are produced, written and directed by Spirit. We are the stars of these productions, and our personal challenges serve as themes. Meanwhile, symbolic messages are illuminated within the spotlight.

To understand our dreams, we need to ask ourselves only one question: what does it mean? It isn't necessary to remember every detail. It isn't important to have complete clarity on those we do recall. Spirit will help us retain important information and discard anything confusing that could complicate our message. All we need to do is recognize Divine Intelligence at work, while remaining open and willing to discover the truth it is trying to express.

Dreams carry messages that might otherwise become lost among the clutter of everyday life. They speak to issues we need to, but may not want to address. As with every message Spirit sends us, we will understand our dreams when, and only when, we are ready to embrace their true meanings.

In this case, Spirit kept telling me the same story. But I wasn't ready to embrace the truth. This is what happened when I tried to analyze my way to an answer.

I'm at summer camp. It's late at night and I'm leading a group of people down Bathhouse Road. Suddenly, my vision blurs and I can hardly see. As I continue walking, each step takes me deeper into blindness. Despite my affliction, I reach the bathhouse, unlock the door and open it for the people behind me.

Like 'The School Dream', 'The Blind Dream' was a long-running series built around a spiritual message. During its ten-year existence, it found me practically everywhere doing just about everything: walking alone through the woods, driving down an unfamiliar road, or piecing together a job interview outfit from old, mismatched clothes I had outgrown. No matter what the scenario, every blind dream revolved around a common theme: my deteriorating vision.

I began having 'The Blind Dream' shortly after graduating from college. At first, it happened a few times a year. But as time progressed, it began to occur more frequently – once a week, then three times a week, and sometimes as often as every other night. Eventually, it reached the point where almost every dream was 'The Blind Dream'. Having by then lost all interest in sleeping, I drank coffee, listened to dance music and exercised before bed, hoping to postpone it.

My dream had me more than concerned; it terrified me. Ironically, while it was in progress, I remained calm and composed. Afterward, it was a different story. My heart pounded and my body shook. My palms were cold and wet. I thought my dream foreshadowed my future.

Spirit's dramatic efforts to touch my soul had only stirred an anxiety-stricken mind. My brain convinced me there was only one logical explanation for having 'The Blind Dream'. I was going blind. Otherwise, why would Spirit keep telling me the same story? No matter the circumstances, each episode featured me squinting at blurry shadows in varying degrees of darkness. Blindness was the only thing that made sense.

Meanwhile, life away and apart from my 'night mirror' had become its reflection. I couldn't see where I was going. Although I had spent the past five years determining where my life was headed, I had never arrived at a career path. Broadcast or print journalism? Public relations? Advertising? My job hunt was taking me in circles.

I continued investigating leads, although none of them felt right: radio disc jockey, public relations director for a cruise ship, hotel receptionist and advertising copywriter. The more I searched for direction, the more lost I became.

Between self-induced insomnia and my unsuccessful job search, I was exhausted. Although I needed to sleep, my mind was racing; I couldn't slow it down. One evening, I decided to make myself quiet. I skipped my coffee, turned off the stereo and darkened my room. Then I put on my most comfortable pajamas, climbed into bed and closed my eyes. Before I allowed Spirit to carry me into my dreams, I asked a question. 'Please tell me what I need to know about my life,' I requested.

The next morning I awoke to chirping birds and the sun streaming through my window. If anything divine had transpired while I slept, I was unaware of it. I didn't remember dreaming.

As I drank coffee and wrote in my journal, a sudden impulse made me put down my pen. Before I knew it, I was dressed and heading out the door.

It was the perfect time for a walk. The neighborhood was quiet and still, and so was my mind.

I continued walking and started to remember something: a dream from the night before. It was as if a movie was playing inside my head. People were reaching out to me, asking for my help. I was comforting them, reassuring them that they were not alone. All the while, my eyes were open and I could barely see.

Although I knew Spirit had spoken, my message was unclear. What did blindness have to do with helping people?

Unfortunately, I was not ready to know my answer.

It wasn't until years later that I discovered the meaning of the 'The Blind Dream'. When I began my life's work, I understood what Spirit had been trying to tell me. My dream had symbolized my purpose and responsibility as a spiritual healer. By using my insight, I help others to see truth.

***

Preparing to Receive Divine Guidance

When we are ready to understand our dream, we may ask Spirit to help us discover its meaning. This isn't the time for thinking, analysis or even interpretation. All we are doing is allowing the answer we already know to surface.

There are many ways to phrase the question, 'What does this mean?' We may ask, 'How does my dream relate to my life?' or 'What truth is my dream expressing?' or 'What is my dream really telling me?' As long as we are open to receiving guidance, Spirit will guide us to our answer.

Once we have made our request, we must trust our inner guidance to reach us. It may happen immediately upon asking our question. A sudden thought, feeling or impression may enable us to make a connection between our dream and the situation it symbolizes. Or, while we are unwinding after a hectic day, the dream we couldn't understand a week ago may suddenly make sense. As long as there are no expectations or limitations placed on how our truth will manifest, we will be able to recognize it when it does.

Inviting Spirit into our Quiet

In a quiet space and in a comfortable position, begin breathing slowly and deeply. Imagine each breath you take fills you with light, and as you exhale, envision negativity exiting from all of who you are. Continue breathing in light and exhaling darkness. Know that the light you are is the Divine Intelligence of Spirit.

Imagine: Light is streaming through the windows of a beautiful room. It is quiet, and we hear someone softly knocking at the door. As we open it, we see Spirit and invite him inside to visit.

He quietly walks through the door and gives us a beautifully wrapped package. Attached to it is a note that reads, 'Here is the gift you have requested. I know it's what you need. You may open it whenever you are ready. All my love, Spirit.'

We open the box, and light beams in every color of the rainbow illuminate the room. Spirit reaches into it, shapes the light into a beautiful configuration and gives us our gift. 'This is your answer,' he says. 'When you are ready, you will see it. Until then, know you are holding it in your hands.'

Expressing our Gratitude

Dreams are gifts that can help us recognize and understand our spiritual truths. They deliver messages that remind us to conduct our life as our true spiritual self. Sometimes, we immediately understand them. Sometimes, it takes time for their meanings to reach us. Sometimes, our answers need to remain a mystery, until we are able to embrace them. Whether or not we understand their meanings, dreams are gifts from Spirit and we must receive them with gratitude.

When we thank Spirit for our messages, we must do so in a quiet state of being. Anxiety, fear, doubt, frustration or any other negative emotion must be absent from our energy. Expressing our gratitude can be accomplished through prayer, meditation, writing Spirit a thank you note, quietly speaking to Spirit when we are alone or through any other means that feels comfortable.

By saying 'Thank you', we are stating appreciation for the information we have received, while at the same time indicating our willingness and readiness to accept additional guidance.

Interpreting our Dreams

Discovering our dream's true meaning can be simple. All we need to do is fit together individual details of our 'story', consider the meaning as a whole and allow Spirit to guide us to our answer.

The following guideline offers a suggestion for dream interpretation. Remember, this is only a suggestion. Spirit will assist us in finding the best way to understand our dreams.

- Tell the story
- Focus on the striking details
- What do we see?
- What is Spirit saying?
- Why is Spirit saying it?

1. Tell the story: Whether or not we are involved in the dream, we need to address it as if we are watching a television show or movie in progress. We want to describe what we see, what is happening, who is involved, and where it is taking place. We may quietly consider the story in our mind, talk it over with a friend, write it down, or use whatever method allows us to clearly and effectively express what we see.

2. Focus on the striking details: Spirit will help us zero in on whatever holds meaning for us, by illuminating our dream's key features: dialogue, colors, temperature, sounds, feelings, setting, time of day and/or year. What information immediately stands out in our mind? What aspects of our dream are most memorable?

3. What do we see? As we remember our dream, what do we notice happening from a literal standpoint, without trying to assign meaning to anything? This question asks us to be a witness to whatever is taking place.

4. What is Spirit saying? During meditation, prayer or any situation that represents quiet to us, we need to ask Spirit what situation our dream symbolizes. Then, once we have asked our question, we must let go (no thinking, analyzing, rationalizing) and trust our answer to reach us. Again, we may receive an immediate response. Or it may take some time for us to access our answer. In either case, there is no need to figure things out. Spirit knows our answer. By letting go, we are creating room for it to emerge.

5. Why is Spirit saying it? Our dream is making a statement about our truth. How does it relate to what is happening in our life? What is it telling us about ourselves with regard to a current situation, challenge, problem or concern? Remember, Spirit knows our answer. Once we ask our question, we must trust our answer to surface when we are best prepared to receive it.

The following examples (my own) demonstrate how to interpret dreams using the guidelines listed above.

'The Car Dream'

1. Tell the story: A woman is driving her car up a steep embankment. There are many packages in the backseat. The car has flipped over and packages addressed to other people are falling out of open windows, onto the ground.

2. Focus on the striking details: The woman is driving up a

cliff; she's alone; packages addressed to other people are in the backseat; the car has flipped over.

3. What do we see? A woman is carrying things that don't belong to her, while trying to move forward to a higher place. But her car has become unbalanced and flips over. Now she is unable to go anywhere.

4. What is Spirit saying? The dream speaks to spiritual ascension, as symbolized by the woman trying to drive forward to higher ground. Spirit is saying that she is carrying too many energies that don't belong to her (packages addressed to other people) so spiritual ascension is not possible.

5. Why is Spirit saying it? Spirit is showing me how I am conducting my life. I am unbalanced because I am trying to carry things (energies) I do not own. As a result, I cannot move forward and will remain exactly where I am.

'The Hallway Dream'

1. Tell the story: Rachel and I are standing in the hallway, outside the classroom. The bell is ringing; class is about to start. She is walking into the classroom and I am following her. But she says I can't come with her and must wait in the hallway.

2. Focus on the striking details: Rachel and I are in school; she won't let me come to her class. I must wait alone in the hall.

3. What do we see? I want to go to class with Rachel, but she is attending it without me. I am waiting outside the classroom until the lesson is over.

4. What is Spirit saying? This dream symbolizes learning. It makes the point that my friend needs to learn her lesson, while I need to remain outside her situation (in the 'hallway').

5. Why is Spirit saying it? Rachel has been enduring a painful divorce. As much as I want to solve her problems for her, I must let her learn her own lessons.

'The Surgery Dream'

1. Tell the story: I am eating wing nuts, bolts and screws for dinner. But I've just remembered I'm scheduled for kidney surgery tomorrow morning. I'm calling to cancel my appointment, because I don't want the doctor to find out.

2. Focus on striking details: eating wing nuts, bolts and screws, canceling kidney surgery.

3. What do we see? I am voluntarily eating harmful, inedible, indigestible things. At the same time, I'm scheduled to have surgery performed on my kidneys.

4. What is Spirit saying? This dream represents self-abuse. Wing nuts, screws and bolts symbolize things that are dangerous to ingest – negativity. The kidneys represent the body's area of elimination. The doctor is Spirit, the Healer. Instead of eliminating negativity from my energy, I am accepting it. There is no point in having Spirit heal me, if I am unwilling to take care of myself.

5. Why is Spirit saying it? I am feeding myself negativity, instead of nourishing my soul in positive ways. I am spending time with individuals who have a negative outlook on life. I need to take care of myself by adopting the energies of positive, hopeful people.

'The Washboard Dream'

1. Tell the story: People are dumping their dirty laundry into a pile in the backyard, next to my old, rusty, broken washing machine. I'm using an old-fashioned washboard to scrub old, set-in stains from their clothes.

2. Focus on striking details: other people's laundry, dumping it in my backyard, washing stained clothes by hand, broken washing machine.

3. What do we see? Everyone is leaving their dirty laundry at my house. I am washing it by hand because my machine doesn't work. All of the clothes are badly stained; none of them are mine.

4. What is Spirit saying? This dream symbolizes trying to

solve other people's problems (cleaning stained clothes I do not own). It literally and figuratively shows me getting personally involved in a situation that is not my responsibility (getting my hands into the dirty laundry).

5. Why is Spirit saying it? I am becoming personally involved when it comes to helping others solve their problems. Their challenges do not belong to me. I am allowing people to 'dump their problems in my yard'. I am assuming other people's responsibilities by cleaning up a mess I did not create.

Dreaming our Answer

Spirit is our ever-present partner, always guiding us to good. Wherever we are, whatever we are doing, Divine Guidance is lighting our way to truth. Whether we desire to view life from a higher perspective, solve a problem, or make a decision that best reflects our authentic self, spiritual assistance is within our reach, even as we sleep.

Requesting Divine Guidance through our dreams is simple. All we need to do is ask. Keep in mind that in order to do so, we must be quiet and open to receiving spiritual information. This means that our last activity before sleep needs to be peaceful, such as prayer, meditation, offering gratitude for life's blessings, writing positive affirmations, listening to beautiful music, reading inspirational books or magazines, or recalling comforting memories. Anything that soothes the soul will bring us peace.

At the same time, we must avoid all forms of negativity: controversial discussions, arguments, upsetting or violent programs, news and newspapers. We must also be free of disquieting thoughts, concerns, fear, judgment and anger. Remember, whatever is in our mind can be programmed into our dreams.

Once our mind is quiet, we may ask to dream about our answer in a clear, gentle way. Our request needs to be a simple direct statement or question that addresses only one concern. For example, 'Spirit, please tell me if my relationship is headed in the right direction' or 'Could you please advise me on how I can communicate better with my son?' Remember, the answer we receive will only be as clear as the question we ask.

If our question contains many details, is too complicated or carries an expectation as to how Spirit will answer it, the result will be equivalent to an unedited, plotless film that is impossible to follow. Spirit knows how to design a dream around our answer. All we need to do is clearly communicate our request and trust that it will be acknowledged.

There are many ways to request a dream. Before we go to sleep we may write a note, asking for guidance regarding a specific challenge, and leave it on the nightstand. During meditation or prayer we may ask for spiritual assistance. Whatever feels right to us is the best way to communicate our request. All we need to do is trust Spirit to tell us the truth.

In the following story, Spirit provided me with my answer. All I needed to do was ask the question.

I was taking an evening shower, when the silent conversation began.

When the Spirit Speaks… Silent Voices of the Soul, whispered the voice from deep within me. I knew I needed to write down the words but ignored my intuition.

You'd better write it down, Spirit warned me, having read my mind.

'OK, OK, when I get the chance,' I telepathically replied.

Now, it strongly suggested.

Finally, I did as I was told.

Soap covered, I emerged from the tub. Then, grabbing a towel with one hand and a pen with the other, I wrote what Spirit had told me to remember on the back of an old birthday card.

At first, however, I forgot the words. When the spirit speaks the silent language? When silent voices speak to the soul? The secret language of the silent voice? It took many attempts for me to get it right. Eventually, after I stopped thinking about them, the right words returned to me: *When the Spirit Speaks... Silent Voices of the Soul.*

Relieved without knowing why, I finished taking my shower. As I rinsed myself off, I tried to figure out why Spirit had whispered those words. Whose Spirit is speaking? What are the silent voices of the soul? How many are there? Although I knew my answers were somewhere inside me, in that moment they were unreachable.

Picking up the card, I carried it to my bedroom. Wrapped in a towel, I sat on my bed, holding it in my hands. My soul knew why I had written down those words; my brain didn't have a clue.

I closed my eyes to clear my head. In my peaceful state, I focused on my blessings. There were many: my family and friends, good health, my healing work... The more I concentrated on life's wonderful things, the more I found others for which to be grateful.

In my quiet frame of mind, I placed the card on my nightstand and climbed into bed. Before I succumbed to sleep, I asked Spirit a question: 'Why did I write those words?'

I awoke the next morning feeling well rested and peaceful. Sitting in my favorite chair and slowly sipping my coffee, I began to welcome the new day.

It was Saturday. My husband had gone to the public market, and my three-year-old son was watching cartoons. The house was a mess. There were dishes in the sink. Papers were scattered throughout the living room. Laundry was overflowing from the wash basket.

Fortunately, in my state of being, nothing could disturb me.

Getting the house in order relaxed my body and quieted my mind. While I was mopping the kitchen floor, I suddenly remembered my dream from the previous night.

Set in a hospital, it featured me, strapped to a table. There were doctors and nurses around me. Someone was holding me down to administer an injection. Someone else was stroking my hair, attempting to keep my focus off the needle that was penetrating my arm. Then I heard a whisper, 'Sodium pentathol. It will help her sleep better.'

Had there been more details to my dream, panic obliterated them. My thoughts immediately raced into the dark. 'I'm sick! I'm so sick I need surgery,' my logical mind tried to convince me.

Fortunately, a spot on the floor sidetracked my thinking. It was dime-sized but big enough to redirect my thoughts. As I scrubbed it away, my negativity began to dissolve as well. At the same time, I began to calm down.

Although the spot was long gone, I continued mopping. The mindless activity not only soothed me, but also freed insight I had locked inside my soul.

Out of nowhere, two quotes I hadn't thought about in years suddenly took center stage in my head: *To thine own self be true* and *The truth shall set you free*. Moments later, I remembered that sodium pentathol was truth serum. Then a book I had never seen, but whose title was familiar, appeared in my mind: *When the Spirit Speaks: Silent Voices of the Soul*. This time my name was beneath it.

'Why did I write those words?' I had asked. Spirit had helped me solve the mystery. They belonged to a book I would write, a book about truth.

***

A special note about the title

Shortly after I had finished revising my manuscript, Spirit sent me a message. It happened while I was talking with my mother. She was telling me that she had been having psychic visions, the same one repeatedly. As she described her most recent experience, chills traveled through my entire body.

Mom's story was brief. It was about a group of people who were whispering, 'Have you read Silent Voices?'

From a logical standpoint, this made no sense. The title of my book was the one Spirit had whispered to me. For the past twelve years I had been holding onto the exact name I had been given. But I paid attention to her words; I held her vision in my heart. My mother is a gifted metaphysician. I knew that she had shared this information for a reason.

As it turned out, two weeks after our conversation, the meaning of her vision made itself known. One day, an idea surfaced out of nowhere; I decided to conduct a book title search on the internet. What I saw on the results page shocked me; 'When the Spirit Speaks' was next to someone else's name!

I couldn't stop staring at the screen. I couldn't believe that the first half of 'my' book title had been taken. I didn't know what to do.

It wasn't until the following day that Spirit was able to reach me. In a quiet moment, I remembered my mother's vision; suddenly, its meaning became clear. Mom had been given the shortened version of what would be my book's first name: *Silent Voices of the Soul.*

***

While we dream, Divine Intelligence is at work, answering our questions, helping us solve our problems, and taking us to school to teach us lessons we must learn. There is always a connection between what is happening while we sleep and what is taking place in our life. Spirit will show it to us as long as we are ready and willing to know the truth.

Even if a dream is filled with bits and pieces of disjointed information, there is always a reason behind it. Sometimes it is as simple as Spirit demonstrating the negative repercussions of watching a violent movie before bed, or the after-effects of carrying worries into our sleep-state. Sometimes Spirit provides a precognitive dream as a warning or preview of events to come. Dreams always have something to tell us.

Whether our drama involves riding the bus to school barefoot, flying to the moon, or sailing through choppy waters, Spirit will help us discover its meaning.

It may happen right away. It may happen while we are running with our dogs in the park. It may announce itself as a song on the radio or appear as today's newspaper headline. Regardless of how or when our answer appears, it is important that we remember something. It is something we are already holding within the light of our soul.

Chapter 5

Energy

I remember listening to music with my eyes closed. It was Halloween and the teacher was playing records for my third-grade class. Our assignment was to listen carefully and notice how they made us feel. But even before then, I had tuned into every sound around me: classmates whispering, a leafless tree scratching against the window, footsteps in the hallway, and the clock ticking overhead. Each rhythm had its own vibration. Each vibration made a different sound. Each sound was music.

Every nearby noise faded when the first piece began to play. Eerily familiar, it made me feel nervous; I had difficulty sitting still in my chair. But the reason behind my reaction eluded me, until the teacher revealed its name: *The Sorcerer's Apprentice*. I had recently heard it while watching Walt Disney's film, *Fantasia*.

While I tried to focus on what I was feeling, I couldn't help seeing Mickey Mouse in my mind. Dressed as a sorcerer, he was surrounded by enchanted brooms. Together, they were catching water in buckets as it cascaded from an overflowing sink onto the floor. Faster and faster, they moved to the music.

That record had conjured an unsettling scene. Mickey Mouse was out of character and frantic because water was flooding the kitchen. Meanwhile, brooms reminiscent of headless people served as 'damage control'. I couldn't wait to open my eyes and clear my mind.

Fortunately, *The Sorcerer's Apprentice* was ending and the next piece was about to begin. The teacher introduced it over the initial scratches as *Danse Macabre* – French, we were told, for 'Dance of the Dead'. The title scared me, but not as much as the music.

Violins hummed a dissonant melody, filling my head with visions of a creepy, moonlit Halloween night – dancing skeletons, ghosts and goblins snaking through misty graveyards, and headless horsemen riding their steeds into the darkness. Faster and louder the music played and everything in my head matched its quickening pace. Then the trumpet sounded; the rooster in my mind crowed to the rising sun. Halloween was over, and everything that had emerged from the night disappeared into the dawn of day.

I have always remembered that music and how it inspired me to invent scary things in my head. Even now, every Halloween, when pumpkins are sitting on porches and skeletons are hanging on doors, *Danse Macabre* still plays from somewhere deep inside me.

Just recently, while I was writing this story, I heard it softly playing in the background of a TV mystery. Recognizing it immediately, I closed my eyes, put down my pen and allowed *Danse Macabre* to transport me back through time.

Suddenly, skeletons and goblins emerged from memory and danced inside my head. I was eight years old again, listening to scary records in school – feeling the power of music.

***

Imagine: Everything in the universe has been set to music. What, exactly, would we hear? Would our thoughts sound like a symphony, or a grade school band warming up in the gym? Would our mood sound like wind chimes dancing in a soft, steady breeze, or fingernails dragging across a blackboard? What would our hopes sound like? What would our fears sound like? What would our life sound like?

There is 'music' in everything, everywhere – vibrations we sense, whether or not we can hear them. We may not call it by name, but we know it well – energy: the life force of all that is.

Always subject to change, its forms are innumerable. It is a thought, a word, a drop of water, the tumultuous sea, the first scent of rain after a harsh, long winter, spontaneous laughter, the serenity of silence, a rainbow shrouded in mist against the post-storm sky… Anything and everything is energy.

Like all things in the universe, we carry within us our own unique vibration – the song Spirit sings from the depths of our soul. This energy is our essence – our true identity. It is the light within us that holds the truth of who we are.

Positive energies resonate with our vibration. They help us to achieve and maintain balance by contributing to our overall state of well-being.

We know which energies support us – the things that make us feel good. Our special song uplifts us. Specific colors comfort us. We are attracted to places that bring us peace. The things we love to do give us joy. Certain scents calm us down. Nutritious foods can enhance our health. Our favorite people make us feel comfortable, love us unconditionally, and accept and reflect our truth. We are in tune with the music that touches our soul.

But not every vibration is compatible with our own. Just as noise can disquiet us, so can negative energies disrupt chords deep within. For instance, arguing with a friend can make us feel sad or angry. Or listening to the news can fill us with anxiety. Negativity carries the potential to cloud our thinking, darken our mood, and distort our perception of ourselves and our reality. It casts a shadow upon our souls, creating the illusion that Spirit no longer resides there.

Positive or negative, we respond to energies according to how we feel when we experience them. What happens when we see the color orange? How do we react when we hear contemporary jazz? What memories are evoked by the aroma of freshly baked chocolate chip cookies?

Our answers are relative. We define energies in terms of how we choose to interpret them. We react to energies according to how our soul translates them.

The next two stories demonstrate these truths.

It was October and I was on a field trip with my Brownie troop. We were at a pumpkin farm; I was having fun. The doughnuts and hot chocolate were delicious. Picking out my first pumpkin was exciting. I was having a good time until I heard the words 'haunted house'.

Unlike the other girls, visiting a haunted house did not interest me. They were excited about walking around in the dark. I felt anxious just thinking about it. The prospect of seeing ghosts, monsters and headless scarecrows was exhilarating to them. To me, it was terrifying.

Almost immediately, my mood changed. My focus shifted from the fun things to the frightening ones. I noticed a glowing jack-o'-lantern; it looked angry to me. Scary music was playing; I heard witches cackling and monsters howling in the background.

When it was time to tour the haunted house, I ran in the opposite direction. A troop leader saw me. Taking my hand in hers, she kept me company while everyone else went inside.

I will always remember her kindness and compassion; I will never forget that field trip.

Recently, John and I took Thomas to a pumpkin farm. He had fun walking through the corn maze. He enjoyed the homemade cider. He even made a new friend; they went exploring together. At one point Thomas pointed out a colorful sign and asked me to read it.

When I said 'Haunted House', a cold chill ran through me.

Jumping up and down, he begged me to walk through it with him. His friend wanted to go too. I told Thomas I didn't like haunted houses; he offered to hold my hand.

Reluctantly, I walked through the pitch-black room with my son and his friend. As I navigated my way through the darkness,

I tried to convince myself that haunted houses didn't bother me anymore. It didn't work. The truth is that they still do.

***

Positive Energy or Negative Energy?

I enjoy camping – spending time with my family in nature and sleeping in a tent under the stars. Every outdoor sound soothes me – the crackling fire, birds singing in the trees, chipmunks scampering in the woods, my boys unzipping their sleeping bags and running through dewy grass. I look forward to swimming, fishing and hiking. I love dining at the picnic table, roasting marshmallows at the campfire and stargazing at night. Camping calms all of me. It quiets my mind, relaxes my body and centers my soul.

While living in nature is an adventure I eagerly anticipate, my sister, Hillary, cringes at the thought. 'Can't you stay in a hotel?' she asks. 'Wouldn't you rather sleep in a bed?' she adds. 'I think you're crazy,' she insists. It's as if we're describing two entirely different experiences. Clearly, we don't share the same perception.

The fact that our opinions differ doesn't prevent me from pointing out camping's finest features. It makes me feel connected to nature. It reminds me to appreciate everything I have. Hillary doesn't hesitate to recite from her own list and nothing on it is favorable: pitching a tent, enduring the elements, contending with insects, and showering at the public bathhouse.

No matter how hard we try to win each other over, our attempts are futile. While camping feeds my soul, it doesn't nourish my sister. My idea of peace is her definition of noise.

***

Every energy holds a unique vibration that, like music, is either synchronized to or out of step with our own. Some vibrations help us to create and maintain harmony. Others can disquiet and unbalance us. Whatever the case, our responses are rooted in how we choose to perceive them.

Thoughts affect and determine our perceptions of everything – ourselves, others and the world. 'Thoughts are things' – energies that supply the blueprint from which we create our reality. Simply stated, we build our life with the energies we carry in our mind.

Since spirit, mind and body are interconnected as one, our thoughts extend into and affect the whole of us. Additionally, because we are one with the universe, our energy flows into the world to collect matching vibrations. Finally, those vibrations return to us as the spiritual, mental and physical realities within ourselves and our lives.

Being aware of energies and their potential to affect us helps us to create internal and external environments in alignment with our Highest Good. Keep in mind that positive vibrations impart balance to all aspects of our lives, while negativity can only upset and disquiet them.

The following guideline offers additional insights:

- We are responsible for the energy we are
- We are responsible for the energy we extend to the universe
- We are responsible for the energy the universe returns to us
- When we have attracted positive energy, Spirit will let us know
- When we have attracted negativity, Spirit will let us know
- We can hold onto energy
- We can release energy
- We can attract the energy we desire by preparing ourselves to receive it

- We can reject negativity by choosing not to receive it
- We can transform energy
- The energy we send out always returns to us

We are Responsible for the Energy We Are

If we desire to be peaceful, we need to create and maintain peace on all levels of being. Beginning with Spirit, we must quiet and center ourselves with energies that calm us: prayer, meditation, hiking, fishing, swimming, reading, reciting or writing poetry, exercising to soothing music... Whatever activity we associate with peace is an energy that will provide us with that vibration on all levels of being.

Once we have created peaceful energy, we need to allow it to expand and intensify within us. This may be accomplished by engaging in rituals that provide us with peace throughout our day.

'Peace rituals' can assume any form we choose. We could meditate or pray in the morning while we are taking a shower, listen to healing music during a picnic lunch, take a relaxing walk after dinner, read a favorite book, work on a special hobby, or think or write about everything for which we are grateful that day. Building times for peace into each day will help us to think, act and be positive. The more peace we incorporate into ourselves, the more positive we become.

Keep in mind that any type of stress can unbalance us, causing us to become negative. Therefore, we must remember to replenish our energy regularly in order to avoid feeling depleted on any level. Should energy depletion occur, due to 'overextending' ourselves, Spirit will warn us through physical signs and symptoms, such as:

Hunger and dehydration – Spiritual message: we are neglecting our most basic needs.

Headache or sinus pressure – Spiritual message: we are over-thinking, over-analyzing, worrying. Too much activity is taking place in our head, creating an imbalance.

Sudden negative mood and/or behavior change – Spiritual message: we feel disconnected from Spirit; consequently, we are attracting negative thoughts, perceptions, and feelings of depression, sadness, anxiety, frustration, anger…

Exhaustion – Spiritual message: we are 'drained of energy'. We have over-exerted ourselves to the point of having no positive energy in reserve. We have neglected our need to rest and are in dire need of it on all levels of being.

Experiencing any of the above symptoms is a warning to immediately replenish our positive energy reserves. It is also a reminder to re-establish balance of Spirit, mind and body by quieting and slowing down to take care of ourselves. This may be accomplished by becoming peaceful through rest, a healthful diet, meditation or prayer.

From a mental standpoint, we create positive energy in our mind through positive thinking. Thoughts such as 'Spirit is always with us' and 'The universe is abundant in all good things' will attract positive vibrations to us. Consequently, positive thoughts send energies of peace, joy and well-being into our total self.

Physically speaking, positive energy affects our body's health. Keeping our internal systems in balance is essential to our overall well-being. It is important, therefore, to eat in a balanced way, exercise in a manner that feels right to us and rest to consistently restore our energy.

In a calm state of being, we lend positive energy to all of who we are. In addition, by thinking in unconditionally loving, kind, compassionate, giving, caring, accepting ways, we create peace, not just in our mind, but also throughout our whole self. In our peaceful position, we can then extend positive energy into the universe.

It must be noted, however, that we are equally responsible for creating negativity within us as well. Forgetting or neglecting to feed light to our soul will make us feel separated from Spirit. Moreover, the thoughts we create in our perceived state of 'aloneness' can only be derived from 'darkness'. Finally, the negativity with which we fill ourselves will spill into all aspects of our lives.

We are Responsible for the Energy We Extend to the Universe

Not only do we create our own energy, but we also control it. The way we choose to react to any situation affects our energy as a whole, as well as determining the type of vibration we send into the world. We are solely responsible for the ways in which we release it.

When it comes to expressing energy to others, we must be mindful of its forms. From a positive standpoint, this may include prayers, kind thoughts, smiles, hugs, spoken or written words of praise and encouragement, and volunteering our time and energy to help people feel good about themselves. By demonstrating unconditional love, support and acceptance toward others, we not only share our positive energy with them, but also empower them to positively impact others' lives.

Offering positive energy in response to something pleasant comes naturally. For instance, when a friend compliments us, we say 'Thank you' and smile. When our child says, 'I love you', we give him hugs and kisses. But how do we react peacefully to less than positive circumstances? More importantly, how do we refrain from offering a negative response in return?

The answer is simple: by being peaceful within. We act as the energy we are.

We are Responsible for the Energy the Universe Returns to Us

This is what happened when I decided to see a situation from Spirit's standpoint.

The day began quietly. I awoke at sunrise to write in my journal. Sitting in silence, I expressed gratitude for all of my blessings. I looked out the window; the trees were still. Birds were chirping; I listened to their songs. Focused on nature, my soul was filled with peace.

While my family was sleeping, I went outside to welcome the morning. It was a warm summer day. Sitting under the dogwood tree, I closed my eyes and breathed the air. The deeper I breathed, the more peaceful I became.

After some time had passed, I went back to the house. My favorite book was on the kitchen table. Opening it to a random page, I found an inspirational passage that resonated with me. It touched me so deeply that I read it again out loud.

All was peaceful and well; I was having a wonderful morning. Later that day, however, I was faced with a challenge.

A letter arrived from Jp's school. I expected it to be good news, but soon I discovered that was not the case. I had applied for tuition assistance. My request had been denied.

For a split second, I was disappointed. Then I sat down and took some deep breaths. When I felt centered, I read the letter again. My perception shifted; this time I noticed something I hadn't seen before. It had been written in a very kind and compassionate way.

Feeling grateful that my son was attending such a fine school, I responded to the 'rejection letter' with a thank you note.

My words were sincere and heartfelt. I expressed how blessed Jp was to be receiving such a fine education. I said 'Thank you' for all the emotional and financial support we had been given in the past.

After I mailed my letter, I put the matter out of my mind. I knew Spirit would answer my prayer in a different way.

Two weeks later, an unexpected gift arrived in the mail. It was another letter from Jp's school – notification that he had been awarded an academic scholarship.

***

We are in control of our own energy. Even when we are faced with a negative situation, we can respond to it in a positive way.

Always remember that, in a negative state of being, we can only release negativity. When we feed additional negative energy (frustration, anxiety, anger…) to a situation, we make it worse.

Again, the energy we are is the vibration we share with the world.

When We have Attracted Positive Energy, Spirit will Let us Know

When our soul is filled with light, we feel centered, happy and good. Through peace and joy we are able to see life in a positive way – who we are rather than who we are not; our wonderful blessings instead of whatever problems we are experiencing. We love ourselves and others unconditionally. We feel connected to the abundant, positive energy of the universe. Grounded in truth, we focus on the good within and around us.

From a mental standpoint, our thoughts stem from energies of balance and well-being, reflecting our peace, joy and unconditional love from within. For instance, 'Spirit always guides us into truth' or 'The universe always supports us' are thoughts born from a positive vibration. Thinking positively fills us with positive energy, laying the ground floor for creating realities based upon our Highest Good.

Physically speaking, positive energy is also demonstrated through balance. When spirit and mind are well, the body mirrors and expresses that reality. Physical demonstrations of positive energy include increased energy, healing of an imbalance within or on the body, or an overall feeling of well-being and good health. When we are aligned with our truth, Spirit will let us know through our body's condition.

When We have Attracted Negativity, Spirit will Let Us Know

In the presence of negativity, our Soul fills with darkness. Unaware of Spirit's presence, we are unable to see or sense our own light. Our vibration is disrupted; our truth is distorted. We feel frustrated, confused and alone.

From a mental standpoint, our thoughts reflect dark feelings. We may become pessimistic, judgmental, critical and hopeless as a result of carrying negativity in our minds. These energies affect our perceptions of ourselves and the world. Due to our negative programming, we view life from a position of 'lack', rather than abundance.

As negative energy, we notice the things we perceive as missing – the holes in our life, rather than the whole that we are.

For instance, we may think we do not have enough money or feel we are not as attractive or intelligent as our friends. These misperceptions could lead us to create and discover more holes within and around us. The more we focus on what we perceive we are lacking, the darker, deeper and larger those holes become. Soon they are everywhere we look. Eventually, they are all we see.

We think of problems as insurmountable obstacles, rather than opportunities for spiritual growth and enlightenment. We dwell on the 'mistakes' and 'wrong decisions' we have made instead of the valuable lessons contained within them. We focus on doubts, fears and frustrations, rather than hopes, dreams, potentials and possibilities.

From a physical stance, negativity can only negatively affect our health. When we are consistently thinking dark thoughts, Spirit has no alternative than to physically demonstrate those energies to us. Therefore, manifestations of negativity will eventually appear on the inside or outside of our body, assuming such forms of imbalance as illness, disorder and/or disease.

Imagine our thoughts are seeds we plant in order to grow our reality. Whatever comes from them can only be an extension of their energy. This means the only thing we can create from a negative thought is negativity.

Too many troubles on our mind can turn into a headache. Circumstances that are difficult to digest can create an upset stomach. 'Carrying the weight of the world' on our shoulders can result in neck and back pain. Buried, unexpressed emotions of anger, shame and sadness can 'erupt' into skin problems.

Even when our body dramatically shows imbalance to us, we still have the option of closing our eyes, covering our ears and looking the other way. Should we choose to ignore the warning signs it issues us, the imbalance we are experiencing will continue to worsen. Spirit will keep raising its voice until we address, correct and heal the real problem beneath the physical surface from where it emerged.

We Can Hold Onto Energy

When we react to energy, we do more than let it positively or negatively affect us. We take ownership of it by becoming the energy of our reaction. Additionally, the longer we hold onto that energy, the more we allow its power to increase within us. As a result, we become a 'magnet' through which we attract similar vibrations.

In the case of positive energy, for instance, after reading a book about making positive change happen, we are inspired to put what we have learned into action. First, we return to the book to reread sections that had the most impact on us. Then we write down uplifting passages to provide us with confidence and strength. From there, we decide to change our career to support our truth. Most importantly, we enroll in a course that provides us with whatever skills our career change necessitates.

Taking a class with like-minded people puts us at ease, offers us emotional support and fills us with enthusiasm. Excited about changing our life, we begin to attract opportunities in keeping with our vibration such as workshops to help us put our new skills into practice and on-the-job training in our area of interest. Then comes our ultimate reward – a friend of a friend offers us the position of our dreams, an opportunity to do the work we really want to do. By holding onto the energy of our book, we have created and attracted realities belonging to the same positive vibration.

Of course, the same rules apply to negativity. Holding onto negative energy in any form will negatively affect spirit, mind and body. For example, if we have ended an emotionally abusive relationship, we may keep ruminating over the critical things that were said to us. The more we hold onto these harmful energies, the more we believe them.

Consequently, as the negativity magnet we are, we attract dark thoughts, deep anxieties and fears. In addition, we feel depressed and hopeless and are experiencing migraines for the first time in our life! We are also attracting various forms of abuse – a reality reflective of our energy. Remember, positive or negative, the energy we choose to hold onto is the energy that creates our life.

We Can Release Energy

When we release energy from one aspect of our being, we let it go from every area of ourselves and our lives. Releasing a single thought causes us to do away with related thoughts, perceptions and feelings. Moreover, letting go of those energies results in the elimination of any physical realities connected to them.

For example, letting go of a negative thought such as 'I will never be a good dancer' and replacing it with 'I am becoming a better dancer' causes us to shift our focus from our perceived lack of talent and ability, to the skills we have and are improving upon.

Due to our new perception of ourselves, our confidence increases, enabling us to join a dance class. From there, we learn new steps and our self-esteem soars. We begin dancing in public. We sign up for dance competitions. We feel better about ourselves, which leads us to improve our diet, exercise every day and ask our boss for a raise. As a result of letting a negative perception go, we have changed our mind; we have transformed our life.

Releasing negativity will also occur at the emotional level. As old feelings such as sadness, depression, fear, frustration, anxiety and anger surface from old thoughts, we can acknowledge them and let them go.

We can facilitate emotional release by writing our feelings down on paper, tearing the paper into pieces, and burning it or throwing it away. We can cry, run around the block, sing, or listen to music that matches our emotions. We can send a balloon into the air to symbolize the letting go of undesirable thoughts and things. We can clear our home and life of whatever energies no longer serve us. Spirit will guide us to our best 'release ritual'. Whatever feels appropriate is the right thing to do.

After releasing our energy, we must also make sure we rebalance ourselves. When we have expressed our feelings, we need to recreate peace in all of who we are. Again, any activity we find peaceful will bring that energy into our being, restoring positive energy to our vibration.

Also included in the release process is the elimination of energies we have stored within our body. Letting go of old thoughts, perceptions and emotions inevitably leads us to physically express them. Depending upon where our old energy has been housed, physical release can assume many forms: sudden aches and pains in our joints (old emotional pain we have felt 'to our bones' expressing itself), throbbing headaches (painful thoughts and memories coming to the surface), crying (release of sadness), exaggerated allergy symptoms such as coughing or sneezing (release of toxins or energies to which we have become 'allergic' or which we can no longer tolerate), or gastro-intestinal upset (elimination of energies we can no longer 'stomach').

If 'illness' or any show of physical imbalance accompanies our emotional release, we should not be surprised as the energies we have expressed spiritually, mentally and emotionally exit the body.

In order to prevent energies from building up and becoming negative, it would be beneficial to build a 'release ritual' into each day. Releasing our energy can include such things as playing sports, making love, cleaning, singing, walking, dancing, painting. It could also involve something symbolic such as weeding our garden or taking a shower and envisioning our stress washing off us and going down the drain. Anything that will help us to release our energy in a positive way will rebalance our vibration.

When our soul has been 'cleansed', we will know it. Our mind will be clear, our body will be relaxed, and we will feel peaceful within. Releasing old energies clears space for us to create our new vibration – one that supports who we truly are.

Releasing the past to correct our current vibration

Holding onto old, negative thoughts and the emotions that arise from them will negatively impact us on all levels of being. Dark, fearful perceptions of ourselves and our lives will prevent us from knowing, not only our truth, but also that of others. As a result of our negative programming, we attract a life filled with energies that oppose rather than support our true essence.

For example, if, as a child, we experienced abuse, we may have been told and shown that love, happiness and respect would never find us. If we internalized rather than expressed our feelings toward those hurtful words and actions, we allowed them to create our reality.

While it is true that the past is over, that may not be the case in our mind. Unexpressed sadness and pain can keep that energy alive long after the event with which they were associated ended.

In other words, holding onto the past means we are giving it permission to affect us now.

If we want our life to change for the positive, we must change the way we are thinking about it.

By getting quiet and allowing Spirit to guide us, we will be able to revisit our past from a positive perception. Our new way of looking at our life will serve to correct our vibration, enabling us to attract circumstances reflective of our truth.

Keep in mind, however, that in addition to being quiet we must be ready and willing to receive Divine Guidance. Therefore, if we hesitate to do the following exercise or are experiencing anger, resentment or any other feeling in opposition to our truth, it is not the right time or the right way to correct our vibration. Only when we are in position to hear Spirit will we be able to receive our answers.

It is possible to re-evaluate our experience in terms of it being our teacher. Consider the following questions: What lessons did we learn from it? What lessons were we able to teach someone else?

In a quiet moment, we may thank Spirit (through prayer, meditation, by letter or any other prayerful means of communication that feels right to us) for providing us with our learning opportunity. At the same time, we can ask Spirit to identify the spiritual lesson contained within the experience. Remember, even though we may not be consciously aware of what it is, our soul is holding our truth. By expressing gratitude for and asking to be made aware of our answer, we are indicating our readiness to receive it.

Once we have asked our question, we must place it into Spirit's hands and trust our answer to find us. Maybe our experience taught us how to love ourselves unconditionally. Maybe we learned about patience, empathy or acceptance. Maybe we were able to learn our lesson as well as teach it to others. Remember, as long as we remain open to receiving our answer, it will make itself known to us in the right way and at the best time.

The following letters are excerpts from my journal. I wrote to Spirit, asking for guidance. Shortly afterward, in a quiet moment, my Higher Self wrote back to me.

> Dearest Spirit,
> Thank you for the unconditional love you give me every moment of every day. Your guidance is a gift and a blessing to me.
> I am writing because I am ready to let go of the past. I no longer desire to hold onto pain – to live my life as a victim. I want to move forward.
> Please help me. I need to see the abuse I experienced in a positive way. I want to be able to see it through your eyes. Please make me aware of the lessons I have learned.
> With all my love,
> Robin

***

> Dearest Robin,
> Life has taught you many lessons – all in the name of unconditional love. The abuse you experienced held a spiritual purpose. You have learned the meaning of 'inner strength'. You have learned kindness, compassion, respect, trust and acceptance.
> You learned who you really are, so you can teach others how to see the truth.
> With all my love,
> Spirit

Embracing our lesson from a spiritual standpoint will allow us to let go of the negative energy we have associated with our experience. By changing our perception of it, we are correcting our vibration and empowering ourselves to attract energies we desire and deserve.

We Can Attract the Energy We Desire by Preparing Ourselves to Receive It

In order to attract positive energy, we must be positive energy. We must create and surround ourselves with vibrations that encourage, remind and assist us in being our truth. Again, spiritual preparation to receive positive energies may include prayer, meditation and spending time in nature. We can also write positive affirmations, create wonderful art and enjoy the company of people who share their positive visions of the world with us. Any peaceful activity that makes us feel good will provide us with a positive vibration.

On a mental or emotional level, our thoughts and beliefs must be reflective of Spirit and our words must also support that energy. Negativity must be absent from our mind, including doubt, anxiety, fear, judgment and criticism. Instead, we need to focus on the positive energies of trust, acceptance and unconditional love.

Finally, physical preparation to attract positive energy requires establishing and maintaining good health through balanced nutrition, exercise and care from medical professionals with whom we feel comfortable. Keeping our physical self balanced will help us achieve peace within Spirit and mind, as well as contribute to an overall sense of well-being.

We Can Reject Negativity by Choosing Not to Receive It

Rejecting negativity employs the same measures we would take to attract positive energy. It is essential, however, to be aware of all its forms: negative and destructive thoughts, depressing, critical, pessimistic and abusive people, self-abuse, substance abuse, prejudice, doubt, fear, negative body language and facial expressions. Remember, the moment we react to something in a negative way, we allow negativity to 'infect' us.

Being aware of potentially negative situations helps us to avoid them. By carrying a mental picture of what negativity 'looks like', we may think twice before allowing it into our energy. For instance, visualizing a bottle of poison with a skull and crossbones on its label is a dramatic representation of negativity, as well as a whirlpool in the midst of rapids, and 'Keep Out' and 'Danger' signs. Anything we can do to distance ourselves from negativity will help us to maintain our positive energy, no matter the situation.

We Can Transform Energy

While we may not have control over our circumstances, we can control how we react to them. When faced with a challenging situation, we have a choice: responding out of frustration, anxiety, fear or anger and ultimately creating more negativity, or changing its vibration by being positive.

When we are anxious or fearful, we can breathe slowly and deeply while thinking calm thoughts such as 'All is well' or 'Spirit always guides us into Good'. We can offset depression and sadness by bringing the uplifting energies of music, books and art into our vibration. We can take a walk or engage in another form of exercise such as dance or yoga. We can also make other positive changes such as balancing our diet, having something fun to look forward to each day, and learning something new to expand our mind. Embracing positive energy in any form will positively affect our imbalanced vibration.

Another way of transforming the energy of a trying or unpleasant situation is to react to it in a positive way.

Here is a story that shows how it can be done.

Thomas was angry. His screaming and crying were almost too

much for me to bear. I had turned down his request to have chocolate for dinner. He was threatening to smash juice glasses. The louder he screamed, the more I wanted to cry.

Lifting my three-year-old son from the kitchen counter, I placed him on the floor. This made him angrier. He screamed more loudly.

I was on the verge of having my own tantrum.

Frustrated, I sat on a chair and took some slow, deep breaths.

In the noise, it helped me to feel peaceful. I continued breathing this way. As I started to quiet down, I realized something. I needed to help Thomas become peaceful.

Recognizing Spirit's whisper, I sat down on the floor next to my son. I spoke to him softly, even though he was crying too loudly to hear me. I handed him a glass of water. He handed it back to me. I offered him his favorite teddy bear. He cried even more loudly.

Having exhausted my resources, I took some slow, deep breaths to center myself. Amazingly, my son followed my lead. Thomas started breathing slowly and deeply with me. A few minutes later his energy shifted; he wasn't crying as loudly as before. Eventually, the tears stopped flowing.

Placing my hand on his shoulder, I smiled at him. I kissed his forehead and he hugged me in return. Then, as if nothing had happened, Thomas picked up his harmonica and started playing it. My son was peaceful again.

***

Recognizing the noise within us is a crucial first step toward energy transformation. Any time we are unbalanced, negativity can find us. It may happen when we're tired. It may happen when we have neglected our spiritual, emotional and physical needs. It may occur when, despite our best intentions to 'go with the flow' of life, we allow ourselves to become swept into a self-created current of frustration, anxiety or fear. Our energy can become negative for any number of reasons, none of which matter. What is important is knowing how to change it back into a positive vibration.

By centering ourselves in peace, we not only maintain our positive vibration, but also hold the power to transform the energy of an unpleasant situation.

This is how I came to understand the meaning of those words.

Thomas and I were waiting for his bus, when he started crying. I asked him what was wrong. He said he didn't know. Everything seemed to be going well at school. He was enjoying kindergarten. He loved his teacher. He looked forward to going to class every day. I couldn't understand why he was sad.

For some reason he didn't want to leave me.

When the bus turned onto our street, Thomas grabbed my hand. When it stopped in front of our house, he begged me to let him stay home. We walked to the bus together. I told him that I loved him. I reassured him that everything was going to be all right.

As soon as the bus pulled away, I called his teacher. I wanted to know if she had noticed anything different about Thomas. I asked her if anything out of the ordinary had happened in the classroom. She assured me that everything was fine; Thomas had been doing well. He had just been feeling a little sad lately. Sometimes, his eyes would well up with tears. He would look like he was going to cry. She attributed his behavior to homesickness; he had told her that he missed me.

The next morning Thomas told me he didn't want to go to school. He asked me if he could stay home. When the bus arrived he started to cry. A pattern had begun to develop. For weeks, this is how each school day began.

One day I prayed for guidance. I asked Spirit for an answer.

The following afternoon Thomas had a doctor's appointment.

I picked him up from school. Immediately, a 'wave of sadness' hit me as I opened the door to his classroom. Focused on getting to the doctor on time, I pushed the feeling aside.

Later that day my mother called. We talked about Thomas. I told her how much he loved kindergarten. I also mentioned the sadness I had felt in his classroom. My mother stopped me in mid-sentence and asked me to repeat my words. I had spoken my answer. My son was reacting to negative energy.

I understood how he felt; I knew how to help him.

Thomas and I had another talk. I asked him why he didn't want to go to school. He said he was happy there, but something was making him cry. He told me that he felt fine until he walked into his classroom. But once he stepped inside, his eyes filled with tears.

Thomas had spoken to his teacher about this; she was letting him do his work in the hall. He had told her that he felt happier there.

Although Thomas was only six years old, I explained the situation in a way he could understand. I told him that he was feeling 'someone else's sadness'.

I explained that I understood how he was feeling, because I felt energy too.

He asked me how to make the sadness go away.

We talked about taking slow deep breaths to calm himself down. He breathed with me. He said it made him feel good. I asked him to tell me all the things he loved to do in school. Math was his favorite subject. He also loved to do art projects, look at books and practice writing words.

I told him to do one of those things the next time he felt sad; it would make him feel better.

It took some time for Thomas to learn how to transform his energy. Eventually he developed a strategy. He took slow, deep breaths when he felt sad. He did math or an art project to make himself feel better. He also came up with his own idea. Every morning he played his toy piano until the bus arrived. The music soothed him; he told me it made him feel good.

One day, he came home from school with a big smile on his face.

'Guess what, Mom?' He said. 'I'm happy again.'

***

How do we return to peace when we have allowed negativity to invade our energy? As always, our answers are within, and in the quiet, Spirit will guide us in a positive direction. In the meantime, the following guideline offers suggestions for transforming energy:

- Breathe to break the energy
- Step away from the noise
- Expand and intensify our peaceful energy
- Become peace

Breathe to break the energy

Breaking the energy means we must immediately stop feeding negativity to our situation. This means, in a heated moment, we must consciously decide to end our reaction. By getting quiet and taking as many slow, deep breaths as necessary to calm down, we introduce peace into our energy. As a result, our mind slows down, our body relaxes, and our vibration starts to change.

Only after we have broken our negativity, can we leave our situation. Otherwise, the negative energy we have created and become will continue to impose itself upon how we think, feel, act and react for as long as we hold onto it. In addition, it will serve as a magnet through which we will attract additional negativity. Once we have accomplished this important first step toward becoming peaceful, we may 'walk away' from our situation, carrying all positive vibrations with us.

Step away from the noise

Ideally, we want to physically remove ourselves from negativity. By doing so, we signal our intention to reject it. This may be accomplished by literally turning around and quietly walking away. Or, in the event that we are having an unpleasant phone conversation, we may politely say 'Goodbye' and hang up the phone. When physically leaving our situation is not possible, there are other ways to demonstrate our desire to create peace. We can turn away from the noise and focus on something pleasant such as a beautiful color, a picture on the wall, the sound of chirping birds outside the window, or the nature that surrounds us. We could just close our eyes to clear our mind, while taking slow, deep breaths. How we choose to distance ourselves from negativity depends upon our circumstances. Anything we can do to distract ourselves from the noise will help us to become peaceful.

Furthermore, we can think wonderful thoughts or recall pleasant memories. We can recite soothing words in our mind, such as 'Peace' or 'Be peaceful.' We can write them down, moving our pen as slowly as possible across the paper. We can also draw symbols such as peace signs, hearts or stars – whatever represents peace to us. Bringing peace into our energy will quiet, calm and center all of who we are.

Expand and intensify our peaceful energy

After bringing peace into our being, we want to expand and intensify our energy. This may be accomplished by quietly scanning our surroundings for things that can soothe and calm us. All we need to do is find a peaceful energy within our environment and allow it to become one with our vibration.

For instance, if we are in the kitchen we can fill a glass of water and sip it slowly. At work, we could take a short break to look at the view out the window, or step outside to breathe the air. In the car, we could turn on the radio to listen to peaceful music. Spirit will guide us to energies that will calm us. All we need to do is be quiet and peace will find us wherever we are.

Become peace

Finally, when we begin to feel peaceful, we can envision a healing white light traveling through us, or a rainbow becoming more brilliant and beautiful with every breath we take. Or we can create our own comforting visualization. Spirit will guide us to our healing picture of peace.

Once we have become 'peaceful', we can hold onto our energy by engaging in whatever quiet, soothing activity our circumstances allow: prayer, meditation, calling a positive-minded friend, taking a nap, walking or driving to a beautiful serene place, playing with our children or pets, etc. The idea is to focus on peace to stay peaceful.

The Energy We Send Out Always Returns to Us

Every thought we think, every action we take, is like a letter of intent we mail to the universe. In return, we receive manifestations of those energies in physical form – extensions of our own vibration.

Within us is an 'energy magnet'. Filled with light, it holds the power to attract every positive vibration we desire to own. Filled with darkness, it can only summon to it every form of negativity imaginable.

Do we desire to invite uplifting, healing energies into our life? Or would we prefer to open the door to every vibration that opposes our truth?

The choice is ours.

Chapter 6

Intention

The picture on the package was impressive but unbelievable – a multi-colored wildflower meadow, swaying in the wind. Beneath it, 'too-good-to-be-true' words promised: 'Be an expert gardener in three easy steps.' There I stood in the checkout line, daydreaming about things that would materialize from my perennial garden in a bag.

According to the package, establishing a flowerbed was simple! All I needed to do was weed the designated area, carpet it with a pink lint-like 'seed mat', water it and wait for breath-taking flowers to grow. Owning the garden of my dreams would be as simple as following the directions.

Planting a garden, however, also required that I take care of it.

Fortunately, only watering was necessary at first. But when green shoots began to emerge, weeding became a part of the routine and my task evolved into a daily commitment.

In the beginning, I enjoyed tending my garden. I looked forward to grooming it and eradicating weeds while envisioning negativity leaving my life. But as spiritual an activity as I tried to make it, gardening soon turned into a chore I avoided.

Not even a month had passed before I was making excuses. Any alibi justified abandoning my responsibilities.

Since it had rained torrentially and continually a few days ago, watering wouldn't be necessary for a while. The following week the temperature had unexpectedly soared; it was too hot to weed. Bees posed an ever-present threat. Lost gardening gloves meant putting off gardening for another time…

Having no one to depend upon, my garden relied solely upon the elements to survive. Fortunately, there had been enough sun and rain for some plants to grow. On the other hand, weeds had overtaken most of their space, leaving just enough room for a cluster of daisies and a few purple coneflowers.

Meanwhile, every other wildflower garden in the neighborhood was flourishing. One in particular had caught my eye. Wondering why it had bloomed so precisely and forgetting why mine hadn't, I asked the homeowner for his secret.

'Oh, it was easy,' he said, pointing to a familiar-looking bag on his porch. 'All I had to do was plant, water and weed.'

***

Intention is more than a decision to create a garden. It is the consistent action we take to bring that garden to fruition. Once we have cleared a space and sown our seeds, we must demonstrate our commitment to help our flowers germinate, grow and ultimately bloom.

As for manifesting that which we desire, the same holds true. While making room for and preparing to receive our reality is a necessity, so is our intention to attract it into our life. Remember, Spirit recognizes both the plan in our mind and the one we physically set into motion as energy. What we think is as significant as what we do.

Every energy within us and every vibration we extend into the universe carries its own intention. This means that in order to attract a situation, our energy must first 'request' it. When it comes to inviting what we desire into our lives, the intent with which we take an action is just as important as the action itself.

My oldest son was the one who first taught me this truth.

When Jp was 11 years old he was intent on owning an aquarium. Ever since winning his goldfish from the school fair, he wanted to give them a proper home. In his eyes, a fish tank was a necessity – something to benefit fish as well as family. He was more than willing to prove his point.

'I like your goldfish,' I said to Jp, who was holding three of them in a water-filled plastic bag.

'Thanks, Mom,' he replied. 'I need to find a container for them… Can I use one of your mixing bowls?'

'Here's one I don't use anymore.'

'This should work. But this is only temporary, Mom. I need to buy a fishbowl.'

'Well, maybe we could go to the pet store later,' I offered.

'Maybe Dad could take me now,' he countered, while transferring his new pets into their temporary living quarters.

An hour later, a fishbowl, special goldfish food and a fish care manual appeared on the dining room table. Before I could examine them, Jp had gathered everything and run upstairs to get his fish situated. Not long afterward, he appeared in the living room beside me, resuming the conversation I thought we had ended.

'Can we get an aquarium?' Jp asked.

'We just bought a fishbowl,' John answered.

'I know, Dad, but I've been reading my manual and talking to friends, and I've learned some things about goldfish. Did you know that they don't live very long in fishbowls?'

'No, I didn't realize that,' I said.

'Not only that, Mom. The water needs to be changed a special way, the pH has to be balanced, and the fish need to feel comfortable in their environment, otherwise they'll die.'

'Oh,' I responded.

'No,' John snapped back. 'An aquarium is a big responsibility… And where would you even put it? There's no room for one.'

'Dad, if you let me have an aquarium, I will show you how responsible I can be. And I know exactly where it would fit – on my desk,' Jp said.

'I have to agree with your father,' I chimed in. 'Taking care of a fishbowl is a responsibility in itself. Taking care of an aquarium is a whole other story. Besides, how many times do I have to remind you to clean your room and take out the trash?'

'Your mom and I need to think about it,' John explained. 'Here,' he continued, handing Jp a phonebook, 'call some pet stores to find out how much an aquarium costs.'

Carrying it upstairs, Jp returned moments later to report his findings.

'Well, I called some stores, and I found out a ten-gallon tank goes for about thirty dollars.'

'That sounds steep,' John stated, giving him the newspaper. 'Why don't you check out yard sales?'

Wasting no time, Jp scanned the classifieds. Newspaper in hand, he headed out the door, hopped on his bike and rode away.

Thirty minutes later he returned, looking disappointed.

'I must have been too late,' Jp said. 'Everyone closed up early.'

Taking the newspaper from his hand, I immediately understood why.

'This is last week's paper, honey. Dad must have given it to you by mistake,' I told him.

Making an 'I can't believe I just rode around the neighborhood for nothing' face, Jp announced he was going across the street to visit our neighbor, Phil. Five minutes afterward, he was racing through the door and into the living room.

'Mom! Dad!' he said, trying to catch his breath. 'I told Phil about our aquarium situation and guess what? He has a twenty-gallon tank in his attic and he wants me to have it, if it's OK with you. So, is it OK with you?'

Searching for an answer, my husband and I looked into each other's eyes. Telepathic communication wasn't happening, so John broke the silence.

'You need to convince us why having an aquarium is such a good idea,' he expressed to our son. 'Make a list of reasons and we'll talk about it.'

Jp, having agreed to do his assignment, handed it to me a half-hour later.

'Here's my list, Mom. Could you look at it before I go to bed?'

Noting the time, I realized that wasn't going to be possible.

'I wish I could, honey, but a client is about to call,' I explained. 'I know how much this means to you. I promise to read it in the morning.'

Sad and frustrated, Jp kissed me goodnight without uttering a sound.

Hours later, he was cupping his hand over one ear, moaning in pain. While enduring an ear infection was bad enough, his discomfort was more than physical. He had planned on attending a party in the park the following afternoon. He was facing the possibility that he might not be able to go. Holding him in my arms, I administered aspirin and eardrops to dull the pain. Stroking his hair, I whispered the answer to the question he was asking in his mind.

'If the doctor says it's OK and you're feeling up to it, you may go to the party,' I said.

As Jp was falling asleep, Spirit whispered the true nature of his ear infection. He wasn't being heard. It hurt to hear 'No', my intuition informed me. At almost 3 a.m., I read the list he had so thoughtfully composed.

Reasons for a 20-Gallon Tank [abridged version]

Gives fish more room to move and play

It's free

Phil will give me his old one

Will free room in Phil's attic – that will make him happy

Will look nice in my room

Will keep me entertained

Will keep me from playing video games

Will give me a reason to clean my room

Will make others happy

Will give me something to care for and love besides my family

My heart held onto his last entry, while my head repeated it: 'Will give me something to care for and love besides my family'. Climbing back into bed, I started thinking that having an aquarium might be a good idea.

Hours later, the doctor confirmed Jp's ear infection, reassuring him that he could attend the party when his temperature had returned to normal. At home, shortly afterward, my son displayed a thermometer reading of 97 degrees (36 Celsius).

It was a beautiful spring day. After we dropped him off at his party, we took a drive through the park.

On the way home, John spotted something and pulled over to the side of the road. He pointed it out to me and chills raced up my spine. It was as if someone had been expecting us and left us a gift: a fully equipped aquarium, filled with bags of rocks and shells.

'The universe supports us,' my husband said, loading it into the truck. I agreed, smiling.

Later that day, we gave Jp his present. Excited beyond words, he jumped up and down. Placing it on the pavement, he carefully looked it over.

'You'd better check it for leaks, just in case,' my husband suggested, dragging the hose over and turning it on. Jp found one as he pointed to the water trickling out of the aquarium.

But he didn't see this situation as a problem. Rather, he interpreted it as synchronicity.

'You know, Mom,' he said, 'I think we were meant to use this equipment in Phil's aquarium. Now, can we look at it?' he asked hopefully.

Impressed with his spiritual interpretation, John and I finally said yes. Our son became the owner of a 20-gallon aquarium; three goldfish had a new home.

***

When we wholeheartedly believe something is true – that what we desire to physically manifest already exists spiritually – our knowing, trusting energy merges with the universe to make our desire a reality. By centering ourselves in peace, believing in our ability to attract what we desire, and demonstrating our readiness and willingness to realize our goal, we are trusting Spirit to rearrange our life in order to support our intention.

At the same time, our intentionally positive energy enables us to clearly request the reality we desire to create. Whether it is the action of thinking or of doing, every intention we express holds meaning. We must be certain that our energy is in keeping with the circumstances we plan to manifest. We must be mindful that the vibration we are and share with the world matches that of whatever we intend to attract.

In order to present a clear statement of intent to the universe, we must take all of our actions into consideration. For instance, if we have decided to change careers in order to pursue our life's work, our overall energy must support our decision. Therefore, if we are thinking about doing our life's work, we are demonstrating a clear, positive intention. If we are looking through the newspaper classified ads for an opportunity to do the work we love, again, our intention is clear. Accepting a part-time job in our field of interest also shows our intention to manifest the reality we desire to create.

At the same time, we must be aware of other energies that may, or may not, support our intention. Are we changing our résumé to reflect the career we want? Or is the old one buried beneath a pile of bills on the kitchen table? Are we researching the type of work we would love to do and meeting with like-minded people who have our 'dream job'? Or are we fearful and unable to move forward? Have we let go of things that no longer support what we see ourselves doing? Or is clutter taking up precious space, not only in the attic, but also in our lives? It is imperative to know what energies our mind, body and soul are holding. It is imperative that what we are saying to Spirit is what we mean to say.

The universe always follows our lead. Here is a story that depicts how Spirit responds to a positive intention.

My friend, Michael, intended to own a hair salon and spa – a healing environment comprising like-minded people whose energies would reflect his own. It just so happened that an opportunity arose to provide him with the space, location and people he was looking for in order to realize his dream.

As Michael established his new business, it became clear that certain energies clashed with the circumstances he had created. Specifically, two co-workers no longer fitted the reality he pictured in his mind. One of them had been verbally lashing out at Michael, making him, as well as co-workers and clients, aware of her anxiety. Another smiled while projecting an 'I don't really like what I'm doing' attitude.

Wanting to give both employees another chance, Michael waited for things to improve. Unfortunately, their collective negativity only intensified with time. When it reached the point where just being near his negative associates was intolerable, Michael made the difficult decision to terminate their employment. Shortly after he let one of them go, the other gave her notice and quit.

Michael felt balanced and at peace after having cleared his salon of negativity. When it came time for him to hire new employees, the universe clearly understood his intention. As a result of releasing two negative people, six positive-minded associates found him.

***

Another way Spirit supports our intention is by making certain we are clear about the request we have made. For instance, after we let go of negativity, it may be placed on our path to see how we react to it. Spirit responds to our statement by asking us, Are you sure you are ready and willing to release the negativity in your life?

Depending upon our reaction, Spirit will know how to support us. If we intend to let go of negative energy, the universe will help us eliminate it. If we choose to invite negativity back into our life, Spirit will interpret our action to mean, 'This is something we want. Please send us more!'

Remember, whether our intention exists as a thought or physical action, it is a statement we are making to the universe; a request we are offering to Spirit to redesign our life accordingly. Therefore, we must be certain that what we are saying is clear – that the collective energies of our thoughts, words and behaviors support the circumstances we desire to manifest.

As long as our thoughts correspond with our goal-oriented actions, Spirit will be able to create the reality we intend to create. It must be noted, however, that if any component of our statement is doubtful, fearful or in any way unclear, our mixed message will be interpreted negatively. That means Spirit must provide us with the doubtful reality we have unknowingly 'requested'.

Below are examples that illustrate the difference between clear and unclear intentions.

Clear intention: I needed dental work. At the same time, business was slow and I had no dental insurance. Instead of thinking in terms of lack (I don't have the money; I can't afford the procedure), I trusted Spirit to help me pay my bill.

I also asked my Higher Self to guide me to ways I could demonstrate my trust to the universe. Many ideas surfaced. I made a 'To do' list, crossing off 'Pay dental bill in full', as if it had already occurred. I thanked Spirit for paying my bill, believing it had been taken care of for me. Despite my uncertain financial circumstances, prayer kept doubt and fear out of my mind.

Just in time for my dental appointment, clients I hadn't heard from in months called to schedule counseling sessions. As a result, I received more than enough money to cover my expenses.

Unclear intention: I had just started my business when my first retainer arrived by mail. It was a $300 check, and while I was thrilled to have received it, the words I used to express myself said otherwise. 'I can't believe this!' I said. 'I can't believe I'm holding a $300 check in my hand.'

One week later my car needed emergency repairs. What did they cost me? Exactly $300! Since it was unbelievable to me that someone would send me $300, it was quickly taken away.

When we intend to manifest a reality, we must clearly express our openness and willingness to receive it. Therefore, the energy we are and present to the universe must positively convey our desire to create that situation.

It is important to note that the action we take toward realizing our dream is only as powerful as the thoughts we are holding at the time. When we trust and believe in our ability to attract that which we desire, our actions will reflect our positive mental energy. Therefore, our combined thoughts and actions state our intention to attract the same reality.

However, if we are holding onto doubt or fear, the reverse is true. The statement we are making is 'I don't believe it'. Since Spirit can only honor what we believe to be true, the reality we desire to create cannot materialize.

My two sons demonstrated this spiritual concept to me in the most wonderful way.

When Jp explained his situation, I knew where the conversation was going. I knew we were headed in a financial direction. He wanted to get a straightening iron for his hair. He needed a new one because the old one was broken. Translation: My son was asking me to buy him something.

'Why don't you get a job and pay for it yourself?' I suggested.

'Mom, I'm fifteen,' Jp said. 'I can't get a job yet.'

'You could do work for people in the neighborhood.' 'There's no way I could come up with that much money. How am I supposed to make twenty dollars doing odd jobs?' 'You're smart,' I said. 'I'm sure you'll figure something out.' 'I doubt it,' he quipped, as he walked out the door. A few minutes later, Thomas appeared beside me. He had heard me talking with his older brother.

'Mom,' he said, 'I need to type some poems.'

'Why do you need to type them?'

'I'm going to sell them. Could you print them out for me when I'm done?'

'Sure,' I replied, thinking he was kidding about selling them. After Thomas had finished typing, I printed his poems. I noticed he had copied them out of a book.

'Thomas, these are someone else's poems,' I pointed out.

'I know, Mom. I told you I was going to sell them.'

'I didn't know you were planning on selling someone else's poems!'

'What does that have to do with anything?'

'It isn't right to sell someone else's work,' I explained. 'That would be stealing.'

After his short lesson on plagiarism, Thomas ripped up the pages I had printed.

'Great,' he announced. 'Now what am I supposed to do?' 'I have an idea. Why don't you write your own poem?'

'I don't know how.'

'Yes, you do. Look out your window and tell me what you see.'

As his words flowed, I typed them into the computer. 'Make ten copies,' Thomas said.

'That's a lot of copies!' I responded.

'I know, Mom,' he said. 'I'm going to sell them.'

Grabbing his papers, his dad and an empty oatmeal container, Thomas raced out of the house. Shortly afterward, he returned with good news.

'Mom, I sold all my poems!' he exclaimed, dumping a pile of money on his bed. 'I knew I could do it. Look, I made twelve dollars!'

Hugging him, I offered my congratulations and told him to get ready for dinner.

'Will you walk around the rest of the block with me?' he asked.

'It's dinner time,' I answered.

'Can we go after dinner?'

'I don't know, we'll see.'

Thomas sensed that I was uncomfortable with his plan.

'It's OK, Mom,' he said. 'I'll ask Dad to take me.'

After dinner, Thomas and John went for a walk together. Jp was with me when they returned.

'Guess what?' Thomas said. 'I made more money. And a teenager gave me six dollars! Look!' he shouted, displaying everything he had earned.

Shaking his head in amazement, Jp smiled at his six-year-old brother. Meanwhile, John helped Thomas count his money. There was $20 on the table; Jp looked at me, stunned.

'Thomas, I want to ask you something,' I said. 'How did you know you could sell your poem?'

Without any hesitation he answered my question.

'I believed that I could.'

***

What is Different

The flowers are blooming

And the grass is greener
The trees are starting to blossom
And there is no snow
And many years have passed and the trees are getting their
Leaves back
The End
by Thomas Vella

Below are examples that illustrate the difference between positive and negative intentions. Remember, every energy holds meaning. Every intention is energy.

Positive intention: To attract an unconditionally loving life partner.

Supportive thoughts: 'I deserve to have a healthy relationship with a partner who supports me'; 'I am interested in sharing my life with someone who honors, respects and loves me for who I am.'

Supportive actions: listing attributes we desire to have in a partner; writing and submitting a personal ad; joining a dating service; taking a class we enjoy with like-minded people.

Unsupportive thoughts: 'I'm too unattractive for anyone to really love me'; 'There's no one good enough for me.'

Unsupportive actions: staying home and complaining to friends about not being in a relationship; declining invitations to meet new people; being so busy there's no time for a relationship.

Keep in mind that any action we take, no matter how positive, will be canceled out by a negative thought. When it comes to creating the reality we desire, expressing fear, doubt or disbelief is like drawing a black line through our request. The statement we are really making is: 'I didn't mean what I just said, so please ignore it.'

Spirit's response then supports our negative intention. We can tell the world we are ready to meet our life partner, but if we don't believe it, it won't happen. We can ask our boss for a raise, but if we think we don't deserve one, it will never materialize. Remember, Spirit can only create what we intend to create.

When we are living intentionally, we are conscious of our ever-present connection with Spirit. Knowing that all things are possible, and trusting our limitless power to attract what we desire, we are certain of our partnership with our Higher Self, the highest creative aspect of who we are.

In our positive state of being, we create a mental climate from which positive thoughts arise. Thoughts such as 'I believe', 'I know', 'I trust' and 'I deserve' signal to the universe our willingness and readiness to create and attract our positive reality.

In our intentionally positive position, we allow Spirit to guide us toward goal-oriented actions. We expect sudden ideas and bursts of inspiration to place us in the right situations at the right times. We know that the events in our life are happening 'on purpose' to support our intention, so we trust Spirit to tell us what to do, where to do it and when. We trust, without question, that Spirit will create the reality we have requested.

Again, we must remember that it is impossible to realize a dream while holding onto fear, doubt, anger or resentment. Consciously or subconsciously, if our intent is negative, so will be the result of our efforts.

I learned this lesson the hard way.

I wasn't sure what I wanted to do, but one thing was clear: I didn't want to be a receptionist. Hoping to be promoted to copywriter, however, I accepted a position at an advertising agency as exactly that.

Meanwhile, I dreamed about being anywhere else.

From my first day of reception work, I felt like an outsider. Separated from the offices on the other side of the wall, I was disconnected from my co-workers. Our divided quarters were symbolic of our relationships. They stayed on their end of the hall; I stayed on mine.

It didn't take long before an 'understanding' developed between us. Although it was unspoken, the statement was clear. Whether it was conveyed through scowls, insincere smiles, or stacks of paperwork being thrown onto my desk, every action meant the same thing to me. I was just the receptionist.

While I pretended that doing unpleasant work in an unsupportive environment was acceptable, my heart couldn't lie. Although I answered phones and announced visiting clients with a smile, after a while my behavior belied a forced facial expression. Having lost my focus, I began to shirk my office responsibilities. I was forgetting to close windows on rainy nights, causing executives to find wet chairs in the morning. In addition, I had forgotten to proofread some of the documents I had typed. One of them was returned to me with a grade 'F' and a note that said, 'Try again.'

Although I had never voiced my unhappiness, my Higher Self was making an announcement: 'I don't want to work here. I don't like my job. Fire me!' But, as uncomfortable as my situation had become, I did nothing to change it. Fear not only held me in place, but also caused me to think there was nowhere else to go. Spirit, having no choice, created circumstances to support my intention.

Slowly and subconsciously, I let go of my job. I called in sick frequently. I stayed home because the thought of going into work nauseated me.

I started making 'mistakes', such as the time I returned from lunch to find what I thought was a mass mailing project on my desk. Unfortunately, I discovered that wasn't the case. A livid media director explained what had really happened. I had jeopardized her relationships with local radio stations by sending confidential financial information to the wrong sales personnel.

Then there was the incident where 30 people were seated in the conference room, waiting for me to serve coffee. I heard a fountain-like noise coming from around the corner. Upon investigating it, I discovered the source: the coffee maker was on and there was no carafe on the burner. I had forgotten to replace it and hot coffee was spewing everywhere.

Finally, there was the time the art director asked me to send her storyboard across town. 'Remember to tell the delivery service to leave it in the garage,' she said. What note had I mindlessly written? 'Attention: Delivery Service – please leave this artwork in the garbage.'

As a result of my unprofessional behavior, I felt the universe pushing me out the door. Secretaries who had been forced to take over my responsibilities when I was 'sick' no longer pretended to be civil. My boss, who had always stopped to make small talk with me, now pressed the elevator button in silence. Company clients who had always been warm and friendly toward me were suddenly cool and indifferent.

Spirit, in the meantime, supported me.

A friend told me about an advertising agency that was hiring. The new art director, who had recently opened a side business, offered me part-time work. And while I was reading the employment classifieds, I spotted an ad for a busy advertising agency looking for a receptionist. It looked very familiar – 'Must be organized and enjoy the work', it noted.

All the signs were there. Spirit's message was clear: 'It's time to get a new job. You will need to look for work. You had better let go of your job, before it lets go of you.' Still unclear as to what I wanted to do, I ignored my Higher Self and half-heartedly held onto it.

Something told me that the next 'mistake' would be my last. But I ignored my intuition and called in sick anyway.

When I returned to work, Spirit proved me right.

I thought I was imagining things when my key wouldn't turn

the elevator lock. When the office manager alongside me had no problem with hers, I began having suspicions.

As the door opened to a rearranged reception area, I knew my changed space foreshadowed things to come. While account executives and secretaries switched offices, and crates of belongings were being transferred from one room to another, I couldn't help thinking 'What's next?'

At the same time, I already knew the answer.

My boss appeared at my desk, asking me to join him in his office. Once I arrived there, he handed me a pink slip and a paper bag for my belongings. Embarrassed, but relieved, I left the room to empty my desk. My 'request' had been granted; I had received what I had asked for.

***

In order to create the reality we desire, we must know and be clear about what we want. We must be able to see ourselves where we want to be, doing what we want to do, owning what we deserve to own. By making our desire a reality on a spiritual level – believing it already exists even though we cannot physically see it – we are inviting it into physical reality.

As I am writing this chapter, I am blessed to be able to share a recent experience that exemplifies intention. It occurred while I was writing this chapter.

Intention to Communicate My Message

It was Jp's thirteenth birthday and we were having a slumber party to celebrate. Most of his friends had arrived, but he was waiting for two more. To pass the time, he asked if he could bring everyone outside to kick a ball around. At 7 p.m. there was still light, so I agreed.

A half-hour later, the last guest arrived. As he joined his friends in the driveway, his father took me aside and said, 'I hope you're not going to let them run around the neighborhood alone.' Trying not to be offended, I reassured him that the party was indoors and said goodbye.

Later, it dawned on me that I had just engaged in one of 'those' conversations. At first, I thought my parenting skills were being questioned. Then I realized that his statement had addressed the questionable safety of my neighborhood. Our home was in the city; his was in the suburbs. He was implying through words, and especially through the tone of his voice, that where we lived was dangerous.

Had I not been caught off guard, I would have politely answered, 'Bill, I wouldn't let my child run around at night anywhere.' Unfortunately, I had missed the opportunity to speak my mind.

Meanwhile, I kept hearing his words in my head.

Hoping I would have a second chance to address the issue, I rehearsed the conversation I would initiate. In my mind and out loud, I practiced using carefully chosen words to say what I intended to say. Then I trusted Spirit to create the circumstances under which this talk would happen.

As the universe would have it, another situation surfaced at the same time, supporting my intention. While reading our local newspaper, I came across an editorial regarding the subject that I had been intending to address.

Speaking out in support of an 11 p.m. curfew that would keep teenagers off city streets, the writer had said, 'We all know how dangerous some parts of our community can be.' The implication and tone of the rest of his letter suggested that some area neighborhoods were safer than others.

Recognizing Spirit in disguise, I wrote to the editor, stressing the necessity of keeping our children safe, day or night, wherever we live. My letter was published. Instead of conversing with one individual, I spoke to the whole community.

***

Spirit is our travel agent –someone we can count on to take us wherever we intend to go. All we need to do is:

Clearly state our request
Trust Spirit to make the arrangements
Be ready and willing to take the trip

Chapter 7

Spiritual Transformation

'And then the day came, when the risk to remain tight in a bud was more painful than the risk it took to blossom.'
Anais Nin

I dug into the compost to bury banana peels and onion skins – to assist their surrender of energies into the earth. Each shovelful of dirt held evidence of transformation in progress: old roots, decaying leaves, eggshells and vegetable remnants in the process of becoming rich, new soil from which life would again emerge.

Suddenly, I spotted something. Bright green and lush with leaves, it offered dramatic contrast to the heap of decomposing dead things in front of me. At first I thought it was a weed, but when I tried to pull it from the ground I realized that was not the case.

The plant in my hand was connected to something – a mound of dirt shaped like a flowerpot. Someone had mistakenly believed it was dead.

I thought about everything we had ever tried to grow. I searched my memory for a name. Tomatoes? Basil? Chrysanthemums? Daisies? Geraniums? I could easily identify all those things; this plant didn't look like any one of them.

Convinced that an answer would arise, but only out of quiet, I stopped thinking to wait for the whisper. Sitting in silence, I began to recall one spring afternoon.

April was almost over when I found them: two dirt-filled flowerpots at the bottom of the basement stairs. I had hidden them behind two folding chairs so the amaryllis bulbs they held could rest in the dark. I had planned to bring them upstairs into the light. Instead, they had remained where I had left them, far too long and forgotten.

Holding onto hope that by some miracle they were alive, I searched each pot for evidence of life. But as I placed a piece of hard, dry dirt between my fingers and crumbled it into dust, my faith started to fade. No living thing could survive so long without light or water, I decided. Carrying both flowerpots to the compost pile, I returned their contents to the earth.

Now I was holding living proof that I had been wrong. One flower had survived. It was possible that somewhere nearby was a plant just like it.

It wasn't long before I noticed the other amaryllis, half-buried in a pile of leaves. Filled with excitement, I picked up both plants and ran to the garage, remembering I had stored their flowerpots there.

As soon as I spotted the two containers, I repotted my flowers and watered them. When I carried them back outside, I noticed something.

At the base of one amaryllis, parallel to the leafy stalk, a tiny, teardrop-shaped flower bud had begun to emerge from the soil. I looked at the other one and found the same thing. Had it been February and the flowers were situated in the living room, this sight wouldn't have surprised me. But it was mid-May and they had endured the elements outdoors.

It was dusk when I brought the flowers inside. I placed them on the dining room table. Whispering encouraging words, I promised to help them grow.

From then on I monitored their progress, nurturing them in every conceivable way. I watered them religiously and rotated them often. I played music and offered them upbeat, inspirational monologues. I even sang to them – anything and everything I thought would support their development.

It took some time before there was any growth. After a few days there was a sign. Although the change was almost imperceptible, I noticed it by comparing both flowers side by side. One of them had become slightly taller than the other.

Like a scientist conducting an experiment, I closely observed my subjects, checking them for any hint of change. As time passed I noticed a pattern. The taller flower continued to grow; its sister had stopped.

Disappointed and intending to help my suffering plant along, I peeled away brown leaves that seemed to be constricting its bud. My efforts only made things worse. Days later the bud fell off its stem. I found it in the dirt.

Meanwhile, the other amaryllis continued to amaze me. Less than a month had passed since I had rescued it from the compost. Now, growing steadily every day, it wouldn't be long before it bloomed.

For the next few days it continued on course, stopping for rest when it had grown as high as the stake alongside it. From there, slowly and gradually, the single flower bud unfolded into three sections, hinting at the shape it was destined to become.

It was early June. The days were getting longer and warmer. The bud was preparing to become a blossom. I had only one concern. We were leaving town for the weekend. I was worried about leaving it behind.

Setting my fears aside, I watered the plant, walked out the door and prayed that it would be all right without me.

When we arrived back home, I raced to the dining room table and realized I had worried for nothing. At the same time I had to remind myself to breathe.

Noting its configuration, I studied the flower in front of me. On each side of its stem were two exquisite blood-red flowers, reminiscent of enormous emperor tulips lying on their sides. One leaned to the left; the other leaned to the right. In the center was a single teardrop-shaped bud.

As I continued gazing at it, the amaryllis became something more. Its full, open blooms turned into a pair of outstretched wings. The tiny bud between them assumed the shape of a miniature head. Before my eyes, a flower had transformed into a beautiful exotic bird.

Admiring my amaryllis, I recalled its arduous journey. I also remembered my own transformation.

For years, I had lived without light; there had been many challenges. With Spirit's guidance, I overcame them. Gradually, as I began to love myself, my truth was revealed to me.

I made myself quiet. In stillness and silence, I thanked Spirit for my gift.

What do you see? asked the whisper from my soul. Suddenly, my perception changed. No longer was I looking at a flower or even a bird preparing to take flight; I was in the presence of an angel.

***

Spiritual transformation is a profound, deliberate change that occurs in stages over time. It is a metamorphosis – an evolutionary process through which we discover truth – the caterpillar becoming the butterfly.

Transformation is a magical-sounding word. It conjures the image of a fairy godmother, gently tapping Cinderella with a magic wand to make her wishes come true. A pumpkin turns into a golden carriage, mice become horses, and Cinderella herself changes into an exquisite princess. Without any transition whatsoever, she and her world transform instantly, effortlessly and dramatically.

If only it were that easy…

Transformation happens because Spirit makes it happen. It occurs when, and only when, we are ready to learn, understand and incorporate spiritual lessons into our life.

The following guideline offers the components of spiritual transformation:

- Willingness to learn
- Willingness to grow
- Willingness to change

Willingness to Learn

When we are willing to learn and understand our truth, the universe provides us with lessons to assist, encourage and support our spiritual growth and evolution.

Lessons can be found everywhere in our life. They are the hardships and personal challenges that remind us to trust, listen to, and abide by our inner wisdom. They are the conflicts that help us to recognize strengths we never knew we had. They are the crises that reorder life's priorities, making us aware of things we might otherwise take for granted.

Sometimes we only need to experience our lesson once, in order to reach a deeper understanding and appreciation of Spirit. Sometimes the same lesson appears simultaneously in different areas of our life, to teach us whatever we need to learn. No matter the case, every spiritual lesson we learn helps us to know our truth. It is only when it has become one with us that no further instruction on the subject is necessary.

This particular lesson showed up at the perfect time and in a perfect way.

I held the phone in a vice-grip to prevent it from dropping to the floor. Almost 20 years had passed. I could still hear my high school driving instructor screaming, 'What do you think you're doing?!' inside my head. Praying my heart would stop pounding in time to hear 'Hello', I waited for someone to answer.

'Johnson Driving School,' said a confident male voice.

'I'm thinking about taking driving lessons,' I replied, trying to stop my voice from shaking.

Next, I heard the company sales pitch, telling me everything I needed to know. Unfortunately, I was too nervous to retain anything the man said. Before I knew it, I was giving him my address. Moments later, I also enrolled myself in driving school.

The moment I hung up the phone another voice spoke to me. 'What do you think you're doing?!' it asked, even louder and harsher than before. This one didn't belong to my driving instructor and definitely wasn't Spirit's whisper. It was the 'me' that spoke out of fear – the one that second-guessed myself. I knew it well.

Fortunately, I had the sense to ignore it. My heart knew the truth: neither chance nor accident had prompted me to make that call – Spirit had a plan. All I needed to do was look at my life to see a higher power at work.

Anyone else would have considered it a temporary and minor inconvenience. From where I stood, my world had been turned inside out and upside down. My husband, John, was in bed healing from an excruciatingly painful infection. My mother-in-law was recuperating from hip surgery and had been relegated to bed rest for an indefinite period of time.

But, as unfortunate as their circumstances were, and as much as I felt their pain every time I looked at them, I perceived things from a purely selfish standpoint. The two people I had relied upon for the past decade to drive me everywhere couldn't take me anywhere. Now I would have to assume responsibility for my own transportation.

Although I appreciated the metaphor and grasped its spiritual implications, the prospect of 'sitting in the driver's seat' terrified me. Decision-making had never been one of my strengths. At the same time, I knew it was a skill I needed to acquire.

It was time to reconsider my place, not only in the car, but also in my life. Pushing my fears aside, I scheduled my first driving lesson.

As my instructor pulled into the driveway, I felt like hiding in the bathroom. Somehow, I managed to walk out of the house and over to the car to introduce myself. Once the preliminaries were over, the lesson began. 'Let's see what you can do,' she said.

Fear wanted me to pray that the car wouldn't start or the lesson would be cancelled due to a freak, blinding snowstorm. Fortunately, I remembered to breathe. 'You can do it; you're ready,' I heard Spirit say, as I started the car, put it in reverse, backed out of the driveway and drove away.

Not surprisingly, what was happening to me behind the wheel symbolized the change that had begun to permeate my life. Little by little, I was inching my way from passenger side into the driver's seat.

From a career standpoint, I had quit my job as a telephone hotline psychic, to start my own business doing the same work for much better pay. On the home front, I was negotiating with the Board of Education, trying to obtain speech services for my son, Jp.

While I was learning to take control of a car, I was taking charge of my life.

For the next three months, I faced almost paralyzing anxiety while I learned how to drive. Eventually, as I let go of my fear, I began to trust myself as a driver.

The day of my road test, I sat in the driver's seat, knowing Spirit was sitting beside me. Minutes later, I was holding a temporary license in my hand.

By the time my official license arrived in the mail, I had started my own business. I had also received confirmation that Jp had been approved for speech therapy.

That day, I opened the door on the driver's side and sat behind the wheel, knowing I could take myself wherever I wanted to go.

Willingness to Grow

When we face our challenge, learn how to view it from a spiritual perspective and eventually release our emotional attachment to it, we grow. Old thoughts, old beliefs and old habits no longer hold us in place. We are able to rise above our circumstances to see their true meaning.

The universe demonstrates our growth by making us aware of things we have outgrown: ideas, relationships, behaviors, careers… Outgrowing our circumstances is equivalent to wearing an old, tight pair of shoes. Life feels uncomfortable because it no longer fits us. And, until we create a new life to support our new self, our old shoes will continue pinching our feet.

As we begin to adopt new, positive behaviors and learn to treat ourselves and others from a position of truth, the universe follows our lead.

Evidence of our healing is exemplified around us. We connect with people who are learning 'our' lessons. Or someone steps into our life to demonstrate our old behaviors to us, so that we can see how far we have come. We also feel compelled to let go of energies that no longer support us, replacing them with those that do.

At the same time, we become sensitive to negative energy. For instance, if we have learned to love, honor and respect ourselves, we have also learned to reject abuse. As a result, any show of destructive behavior, whether self-imposed or directed toward us by others, becomes unacceptable. Not only is abuse 'not OK', it is now an intolerable violation of truth.

Spiritual growth enables us to experience who we have been, who we are and who we are becoming. It provides us with the opportunity to see ourselves through Spirit's eyes.

This experience found me when I was ready to let go of the past.

I couldn't wait to remove the rug from the staircase. It was worn and dirty. I didn't like looking at it. I wanted to tear it off fast and carry it to the road. My chore held symbolic significance. An old rug didn't belong in the new life I was in the process of creating. Footprints reminded me of the past. I had allowed others to 'walk' all over me.

John helped me get the project started. He ripped the rug away from the bottom step. Together, we lifted it up and pulled it off the staircase a little at a time. The rug was heavy and cumbersome. More than once I had to put it down. I had to give my arms a rest before I could pick it up again.

Eventually, we dragged the rug out of the house and left it by the road.

I thought my job was done. But when we went back inside to admire the 'new' stairs, John pointed something out to me. Hundreds of staples had been left behind. They blended in with the woodwork, so I hadn't seen them at first. He demonstrated how to remove them. Then I took over the task.

I had to be patient with the process. I could only work on one staple at a time. First, I lifted it with a screwdriver. Then I removed it with a pair of pliers. Sometimes a staple would come out easily. Sometimes it would break while I was trying to release it. Sometimes it was so firmly embedded in the wood that I had to take it out with a special tool.

There were no shortcuts. There was no way to expedite the transformation. If I tried to speed things up, something would happen to slow me down. Spirit reminded me to take my time.

When I removed a staple in one step instead of two, I ended up gouging the wood. When I attempted to pull one out with my fingers, I stabbed myself. When I tried to move forward too quickly, I tripped.

The process was slow. It took nearly a week to finish the project. Patience, energy and time were required to make it happen. Whenever I removed a staple from the staircase, I acknowledged my progress. I celebrated my success. To me, each staple represented something from my past that had held me in place – an unhealthy thought, a negative perception, a limited way of looking at life… I had let go of many things that no longer served me.

My work had been completed. I walked up the stairs, silently congratulating myself on a job well done. The old rug was gone. So were the staples that had held it down. Light was shining on the staircase. There were no footprints to see.

I was on my way to the second floor, when my sock caught itself on a staple.

Not so fast, Spirit whispered, *not so fast.*

Willingness to Change

As we replace old thoughts and behaviors with those reflective of our truth and we consistently incorporate them into our lives, we change. It happens little by little. We begin to think about ourselves in ways that support our Highest Good and interweave those thoughts into the tapestry of our life.

Our new thoughts allow us to see things from a new perception. Our new perception enables us to create a life with Spirit in mind. Our life changes and our changed life mirrors our changed self.

This is how Spirit showed me that I was in the process of changing.

Before I invited light into my life, the condition of the living room didn't bother me. I didn't see the cracks and holes in the walls. I never noticed that paint was peeling. Now that I was in the process of healing myself, those things were unacceptable. The living room was an extension of my former vibration. It was not a reflection of the energy I had become.

It took a while for me to make the connection. The more time I spent in the living room, the more depressed I felt. I was writing in my journal when Spirit whispered the reason why. The walls were in a state of disrepair. They reminded me of who I used to be.

Changes needed to be made. There was just one problem: I didn't know where to start.

When I asked John for his input, I discovered we didn't share the same perception. He didn't see the need for change. John had served in Vietnam; he was a front-line soldier. His tolerance for uncomfortable living conditions by far surpassed my own.

While my husband couldn't relate to how I was feeling, he offered his support. He suggested that we paint the living room. John agreed to help with the prep work. I volunteered to do the painting. The next day we purchased our supplies and started the project together.

It felt good to remove chipped paint from the wall and watch it fall to the floor. Bit by bit, piece by piece, I was getting rid of something old to replace it with something new. While I was scraping, I remembered the negative energies I had released from my life: self-destructive thoughts, a pessimistic attitude and a belief system based in lack.

Some areas were easier to scrape than others.

There was a crack on the ceiling. At first I didn't think it was serious. But when I tried painting over it, I discovered I had underestimated its depth. The crack showed through the paint. It was also much longer than I realized. It started at the middle of the ceiling and extended halfway across the room. When I scraped away the surrounding damage, an enormous 'injury' was left behind.

The thought of fixing it was overwhelming to me.

For a moment I considered handing it over to someone else. I didn't know if I was capable of doing the work. I wasn't sure if I could stand on a ladder and repair the ceiling at the same time.

A part of me wanted to walk away from the job. A bigger part of me knew I needed to finish what I had started.

My brother-in-law, Chris, offered me guidance. He told me how to fix the ceiling. He reminded me to take my time. 'Be patient. It's a process,' he said. I stood on a ladder and repaired the deep depression. I made sure the plaster adhered to the ceiling, and waited for it to dry.

The next day, I started painting the living room. It was 98 degrees (37 Celsius). The air was almost too heavy to breathe. There was no air conditioning in the house.

In the past, I would have stopped working the moment things began to feel uncomfortable. Now, making this change was the only thing that mattered. I had made a commitment. I was determined to get the job done.

Taking good care of myself was my first priority. I drank water when I was thirsty, rested when I felt tired, and ate healthy meals. I kept a positive attitude. I listened to jazz and rolled paint on the walls to the rhythm of the music.

The heat wave lasted for two weeks. It ended the day I finished painting. As I cleaned up newspapers and pulled tape from the woodwork, I admired the space I had transformed. The room looked brighter and bigger than before. The repairs I had made were barely noticeable. The imperfections on the ceiling resembled faded scars.

Throughout the entire process, I had thought about my own transformation. I remembered the lessons I had learned. While I repaired cracks and holes, I reminded myself to be patient. As I climbed the ladder, I took one step at a time. In the heat, I stayed balanced. I took care of myself – spirit, body and mind.

I glanced at the dining room. It hadn't been painted yet. There were cracks and holes in the walls. Paint was peeling. I took a deep breath. I knew how to make the transformation happen – bit by bit, piece by piece, one small change at a time.

***

'When the student is ready, the teacher appears' and when we are open and willing to learn our truth, we find teachers everywhere. Our teacher can assume any form: relationship conflict, mental or physical imbalance, financial hardship... Whatever disguise it wears, we must recognize it for what it really is, knowing the lessons it has to teach us will be life-changing.

Here are some of the many lessons we learn during spiritual transformation:

- Unconditional love of self
- Unconditional love of others
- Self-acceptance
- Acceptance of others without judgment
- Compassion
- Kindness
- Patience
- Self-respect
- Respect for all of life
- Honor and respect for our physical body
- We are more than our physical body
- We are not the things we own
- We are perfect in our imperfection
- We and Spirit are one

In this story, I learned the meaning of transformation.

I never liked change. To me, it was something to fear and avoid at all costs. Change was the end of running barefoot through warm summer grass and the beginning of chilly air, homework and early morning walks to the bus stop. It was Sarah, my best friend in second grade, moving to Shaker Heights. It was leaving the security of my grammar school and transferring to three different ones, while a new one was being built. Change meant outgrowing my favorite black patent leather shoes and bandaging blisters while I broke in the new pair. It was having my teeth pulled for braces and breaking up with boyfriends. It was getting fired from jobs.

Change was letting go of the things I knew and replacing them with the unfamiliar. It was abrupt; it was disquieting. And no matter the circumstance, it always caught me off guard.

I thought I was having an old repetitive dream – the one where I knocked on neighborhood doors and strangers spoke through glass, telling me all my friends had moved away. I couldn't believe what was happening; my life felt surreal.

It was as if a tornado had appeared out of nowhere, obliterating my own private world, forcing me to relinquish the things I knew and loved, without any explanation. I didn't recognize anything around me.

Transformation had announced itself powerfully and dramatically. It was our two dear friends unexpectedly passing away within weeks of each other, my parents losing their home of nineteen years, my mother-in-law being diagnosed with Alzheimer's disease, Jp's two best friends moving away, our compassionate dentist closing his practice, and my husband losing his job.

Within six months, change had invaded every crevice of my life.

It had happened so fast that, at first, I didn't realize it was also happening to me. Preoccupied with helping my family and friends heal, I was oblivious to my own transformation in progress. The world around me was my reflection, if only I was willing to look.

But I wasn't ready to peer into the mirror; I thought I knew who I was. I was a psychic – an 'energy reader', someone who told people where they had been, where they were and where they were going. Now for some reason, I was beginning to feel that the word 'psychic' no longer defined me. I kept hearing Spirit whisper, *Be more.*

I tried to conduct business as usual; clients were calling regularly. However, it was becoming apparent that I was no longer helping many of them. The signs were unmistakable. Some people were using me as a sounding board to vent their negativity. Others were holding me personally responsible for their happiness and depending upon me to get them through the day. Had it not been for the few wonderful souls who appreciated my guidance, I would have gladly returned to working in the corporate world.

Although I pretended not to listen, I heard Spirit shouting at me – telling me I had outgrown my job and insisting that I discover my life's work. Fear prevented me from trusting the truth, so the universe spoke more loudly. Translation: If a fairy godmother lightly tapped Cinderella to transform her, mine was repeatedly hitting me over the head.

First, I became depressed. Next came the daily, migraine-like headaches. Then there was nausea that persisted for months. My body trembled from anxiety. My face turned red and felt hot. My hands and feet were cold and periodically went numb. But, instead of addressing the real problem, I focused on treating the symptoms.

While the doctor's diagnosis was stress, I knew better. My body was unbalanced and I could feel it to the core. Spirit was showing me the repercussions of forcing myself to fit into clothes I had outgrown.

Not until I had come down with laryngitis was I ready to accept the truth. Being quiet voluntarily was one thing. Having silence forced upon me was another.

There was no ignoring Spirit's message. Repetitive and persistent, it was like a recording stuck on 'replay'. No matter where I was or what I was doing, I had to be quiet. And in my quiet I heard, *Be more*.

It took some time, but eventually the meaning of Spirit's message became clear. I had 'lost' my voice, because I wasn't speaking my truth. I needed to redefine myself. It was no longer enough for me to forecast people's futures. I needed to provide them with spiritual guidance so they could take themselves wherever they wanted to go.

Soon after receiving Spirit's message, my voice returned, just in time for our summer vacation in the Adirondacks.

As I packed our suitcases, my heart filled with anticipation. I longed to see the house that for a week we would call home. I wanted to awaken to clean, crisp mountain air and a fire crackling in the wood-burning stove. I needed to settle into the big, worn red chair to plot our fishing strategies for the day. I couldn't wait to listen to classical music and drink coffee from the mug with the frogs on the handle.

There would be comfort in the rituals and routines that had remained the same for as long as I had known them. Never had I looked more forward to them than now. Deep down, however, I knew reality wouldn't meet my expectations.

We had barely passed the 'Welcome to Indian Lake' sign when we noticed that the restaurant with the carved wooden bear out front had burned down. Across the street a 'For Sale' sign was posted on a car repair shop; its owner had provided us with bait, fishing tips and restaurant recommendations for the past decade. Just before we turned the corner onto 'our street', orange signs warned it was under construction.

I was well aware of the messages, metaphors depicting my reality. There would be no hiding from change, not even in a place I called my second home. The mountains, once my safe haven, had become as strange and unfamiliar as everything else. I knew the mountain house would be no exception.

The first thing I noticed upon opening the door was that everything had been rearranged. The big red chair was gone. The green couch had been moved away from the wall into the center of the living room. Books and bookshelves had been replaced with a VCR and videotapes. Blankets were missing. Pictures had been moved. The canoe that had been stored in the basement was nowhere to be found. The special mug with the frogs on the handle had disappeared.

I surveyed the house that looked nothing like I remembered. Many things were gone. Many things had changed. Sitting in a chair I had never seen before, I closed my eyes to let Spirit find me.

Change is all around you because it has happened within you, said my soul's voice. *You are looking at your own reflection.*

***

Chaos or Change Happening Actively On Schedule?

During spiritual transformation, 'old' things are leaving our life, while new ones are taking their place. It is an eventful and challenging time. While it may appear as though everything has been turned inside out and upside down, remember, there is a divine purpose behind every change that is happening. Spirit is rearranging our life to support our Highest Good.

Any change can feel overwhelming. If we are holding onto fear (or any energy in opposition to truth), it looks like chaos to us. But when we look at change through Spirit's eyes, we see the truth behind our physical circumstances. We see 'chaos' as Change Happening Actively On Schedule.

Here are some important things to keep in mind during times of change:

Remember to trust

No matter what your life looks like, remember that Spirit is in the process of supporting you. Remind yourself to breathe; remember who you really are. Keep in mind that your life is changing to support the changes you have made within. You are moving forward. Let Spirit light the way.

Allow change to happen; fighting it will only serve to hold you in place. Open your fists; release your grasp on the past. Let go of the fear. Let Spirit guide you.

Remember to be patient

Everything is in perfect order. Spirit is redesigning your life.

Keep in mind that transformation is a process. Remind yourself that a seed does not become a flower overnight. Be patient; creating a new life takes time.

Remember to love yourself

Be loving, compassionate and kind to yourself. Find ways to bring peace and happiness into your life: think loving thoughts, make time for quiet, read inspirational books, surround yourself with positive, uplifting people, listen to your favorite music, eat healthy foods…

Remember to stay 'grounded' while the winds of change are blowing. Take care of yourself – body, mind and soul.

***

How do we know we are in the midst of spiritual transformation? Spirit lets us know by demonstrating change. It happens when we get married, get divorced, find a new career, lifestyle, diet, religion, residence, have a baby…

I had just written those words and was expressing my gratitude to whoever had whispered them to me. 'Thank you for writing this chapter,' I said. 'I wish I could thank you in person.'

'Don't worry,' said the voice from within. 'You will.'

Unbeknownst to me, I was pregnant at the time. Less than nine months later my son, Thomas, was born. Now, four years afterward as I rewrite this chapter, my beloved grandmother has passed away – poignant reminders to me that we are forever transforming.

Slowly and purposefully, spiritual transformation happens. We grow. We change. We grow some more and we change again. Each change we endure provides us with the opportunity to experience truth. As long as we are open and willing to learn who we really are, Spirit will teach us all we need to know.

Chapter 8

Transition

Spiritual transition is the time in-between transformation and truth – the bridge we cross to leave our past behind in order to live in the present. It is our baby holding a bottle in one hand and a 'big kid' cup in the other. It is our almost 11-year-old child walking hand in hand with us, until he spots his friend and abruptly lets go. It is the gold-turned tree in autumn, still holding onto a few green leaves – the simultaneous act of waving goodbye to the old and hello to the new.

When we are 'in transition', we find ourselves in-between where we used to be and where we want to be. Having left our former life behind, we have ventured into new territory in search of truth. Sometimes we know exactly where we are going. Sometimes we need our map to help us find the way. Then there are times that we forget we even own one.

This is what my life looked like while I was in the process of transition.

I had just completed my test when the buzzer sounded. Handing it to Judge Judy, I smiled.

'You look pleased with yourself,' she said, adjusting her glasses to examine my work. Shaking her head in displeasure, she looked up from the paper into my eyes. 'My dear, you didn't follow directions,' she explained. 'This test covers everything from first semester until now – and it's an essay, not multiple choice.'

'How can I write about something I don't even remember?' I asked, anxiously.

'Exactly,' she replied.

Before I could ask her to elaborate, I was someplace else – running from the house I had lived in as a child and noticing the school bus fast approaching the bus stop.

Fortunately, the door was about to open. I made it there just in time. As I was standing in line, I looked at what I was holding in my hand – my old glasses instead of my new pair.

Having just stepped onto the bus, my setting changed again. I was walking along the sidewalk near my present-day home. Suddenly, someone threw a sheet over my head, picked me up and tossed me into the backseat of a 1970s station wagon.

'We're going for a drive through the old neighborhood,' the driver whispered as he locked the doors.

Finally, I found myself sitting at a desk, signing an important document. I had started to write my maiden name but was able to change my 'C' for Cohen into a 'V' for Vella. For some reason, I felt relieved that I was able to correct the mistake.

My dreams were warning me to remember the lessons I had learned. They were reminding me that I had changed and was no longer the person I used to be. There was just one problem: I had no idea why.

That didn't stop Spirit from telling me the truth.

Although signs and symbols were in place to guide me, somehow I had managed to bypass them all. I had reached into the cabinet for cleanser, and a diaper had fallen into my lap. I had been sleeping too long and feeling nauseated. I had been crying for no apparent reason. Now I was holding a light-pink stick in my hand.

Still I was skeptical. There had been so many disappointments. We had been trying to conceive without success for the past eight years. John and I had just decided to let go of our dream to have another child. We were in the process of accepting that Spirit had a different plan for us.

Even so, I reread the test directions to confirm that I had followed them correctly. Then I studied the pregnancy stick from every angle and in every light. Any shade of pink indicated a positive result. My stick was pale but unmistakably pink.

Had I not remembered to breathe, I would have hyperventilated. My mind sped toward events to come: holding my newborn, singing him to sleep, watching him take his first steps and hearing his first words.

I wasn't dreaming. My prayers had been answered. I was going to have a baby!

It was only a matter of minutes before fear crept into my thoughts. 'Oh my God, how am I going to be able to handle this?' I asked myself. 'What was I thinking?' I wondered. 'What is this soul thinking?!' I asked out loud.

From a fearful perception, life suddenly looked very different. My husband was only working part-time, my business had slowed down, I was on the verge of turning 40 and my husband was about to become 55. There would be round-the-clock feedings, endless diaper changes, and years and years of sleep deprivation.

As time passed and hormones surged through me, I vacillated between being peace-filled and fear-ridden. 'Good days' were centered in faith, unconditional love and positive reinforcement from family and friends – reminders from the universe that all was well within and around me. 'Bad days' were a reflection of whatever dark thoughts I was holding in my mind.

I hoped my doctor's appointment would fall on a good day. It was challenging for me to hold onto peace for more than a minute at a time. The joy I felt was powerful but fleeting. One moment, I was thanking Spirit for the precious miracle inside me. The next, I was panic-stricken over not being young and not having enough energy.

Fortunately the doorbell rang, breaking my train of negative thoughts. It was my friend, Marlene. She had come to accompany me to the doctor's office and offer much-needed moral support.

Marlene always had a peaceful effect on me. The sky could be falling and the roof might be caving in on her, yet she always exuded calm. Blessed to have her beside me, I felt her energy quieting and comforting my soul.

'This is a miracle, Rob,' she said with her arm around me as we walked to the car. 'Everything will be fine,' she reassured me.

I held onto her words all the way to the waiting room. Sitting down, I stared at the fish-filled aquarium while a knowing energy took over my mind. *Everything will work out. Everything will be fine*, said the silent voice resounding within me.

Just then, a nurse called my name, interrupting my peace. After confirming my pregnancy, she checked my blood pressure and weighed me. Then she escorted me to the examining room where, dressed in a gown that was three sizes too large, I read pregnancy-related pamphlets to pass the time.

The doctor's knock startled me. I was studying 'High-Risk Pregnancies: What every woman of advanced maternal age should know'. I expected him to say 'Congratulations' when he walked into the room. Instead, he launched into a monologue.

'You're thirty-nine,' he said while reviewing my chart. 'You'll be forty when you deliver. Your age puts your baby at risk for severe birth defects, including Down's syndrome. You're going to need amniocentesis, and you had better plan on having another C-section… You don't have health insurance? Good luck!' he said on the way out the door.

Suddenly, the room was too cold and my hands felt numb. My body was trembling and I could barely breathe. I sat down for a moment to calm myself. As soon as I could feel my fingers again, I got dressed and walked out to the waiting room.

'It's official, I'm pregnant,' I said, hugging Marlene.

'Congratulations! I'm so happy for you,' she replied.

Somehow, I held myself together until we reached the car. Then the tears flowed. I tried to attribute them to hormones, but my friend knew something had upset me. At Marlene's insistence, I told her what the doctor had said to me. Meanwhile, she held my hand.

'All that matters is that beautiful baby,' she said. 'Focus on the positive.'

When we finally arrived in my driveway, I grabbed the pamphlets and booklets the doctor had given me – none of which looked the least bit uplifting. Then I thanked her for being in my life and said goodbye.

Once I was inside my house, I glanced at the literature I was holding in my hand. At the same time I remembered the doctor's words. As my head filled with fear, my energy shifted. I became light-headed. My vision resembled static on a TV in-between stations – I could barely see. I felt heat building in my face while my legs tingled with numbness. It was all I could do to inch my way to the couch.

Too much negativity had hit me too fast; I almost blacked out. My mind was overflowing with all the things I needed to do: health insurance to get, prenatal appointments to make, procedures to schedule… I needed to clear the clutter in my head.

Since not having insurance was foremost in my mind, I decided to begin there. The phone book was filled with listings. I figured I would have difficulty deciding which company to choose. What I didn't foresee was receiving a unanimously negative response.

'Pregnancy is a pre-existing condition,' they told me. 'A pre-existing condition is uninsurable.'

It was difficult hearing the words. All I wanted to do was celebrate my pregnancy – to extend peace and joy to the child growing inside me. But it was challenging sending positive energy to my baby, while every door I tried to open slammed in my face.

Taking a pink angel figurine from the window, I held it in both hands as I prayed for guidance. 'I know you have a plan for me,' I said out loud. 'Please light my way so I can see where I am going.'

When I had calmed down, I picked up the phone and called my mother. She is the healer I reach for when the physical happenings of my life require a spiritual interpretation.

As I explained my insurance dilemma, Mom responded without hesitation. 'It's a trust test. You need to let go of the fear,' she explained. 'Everything is going to be OK. Remember, you don't have to know how.'

Almost immediately after speaking to my mother, my sister, Hillary, called. Aware of my circumstances, she offered comforting words: 'Don't worry. It will all work out. Someone will help you,' she said.

Filled with faith and confidence, I returned to my 'To do' list. In a much-improved frame of mind, I called the hospital to schedule my procedures.

The calm in my soul expanded when I heard the receptionist's voice. Her energy was caring and compassionate; I could feel it over the phone. Reassuring me that amniocentesis wasn't as frightening as it sounded, and that the ultrasound test was routine, she scheduled both procedures while I waited for the inevitable question.

'Who is your insurance carrier?' she asked.

'Actually, I don't have one right now,' I replied. 'I tried to get health insurance, but every company I have contacted has told me that I'm uninsurable because of my pre-existing condition.'

'I'm going to give you a number and I want you to call it immediately,' she said. 'There is a grant program through the hospital that funds uninsured pregnant women experiencing financial hardship. I know the woman who administers it. Make an appointment with her to see if you qualify.'

With gratitude beyond words, I promptly called the woman. After a lengthy phone conversation, she asked me to come in for a personal interview to determine my eligibility for a grant. I agreed and made an appointment, trusting Spirit to guide me.

One month later, I was enrolled in the program. But as grateful as I was to be a participant, it was not without its challenges. One hospital-related experience after another would offer me additional opportunities to test my knowledge of trust.

On many occasions my files were misplaced and test results were lost. Every time I came in for an appointment, the same receptionist asked if I was a new patient while handing me forms to complete as if she had never met me.

During my eighth month, an ultrasound test was ordered because the doctor was concerned my baby wasn't growing properly. The day of my planned C-section, I was told I didn't have an appointment; I was sent to the wrong room.

Even while surgeons were performing my Caesarean, I overheard one of them say, 'Wow, it's amazing she ever got pregnant with all that scar tissue!' Then he said, 'Look at this!' without explaining what 'this' referred to.

My frame of mind quickly changed when, a moment later, my seven-pound two-ounce perfectly healthy baby boy arrived. As I held Thomas in my arms, I knew I had passed my test.

***

Transition time is a soul-stretching, mind-bending place of self-discovery. It is the adjustment period we face as we let go of who we have been, in order to become who we really are. It is the equivalent to heading off to school with every book we need for the day, only to discover a giant hole in our backpack. It is when Spirit brings to our attention the lessons we know, as well as those we must relearn.

Spirit administers many tests during our transition – none of which have multiple-choice questions. Rather, we are taken back to the beginning, when we first learned of truth, and sent out 'into the field' to see what we remember. Sometimes we are presented with an experience that tests our knowledge of a single subject, such as unconditional love, trust versus fear, or truth versus illusion. But more often than not, one experience will serve to test us on all of the above and more.

It is a confusing time. We have taken our new shoes out of the box to try them on and break them in. We walk around in them to see how a style we have never worn before looks and feels on our feet. We wear them for a while, interchanging them with our old pair. Sometimes we forget which ones we are wearing.

More than ever, there is profound purpose in our struggles and challenges. Not only does everything hold symbolic significance, but life's happenings are also layered with multiple meanings. Whether or not we are able to recognize their truths depends upon how we choose to view them.

It all comes down to one word – trust. This is the time we repeatedly remind ourselves that Spirit is always holding our hand, because at times it may seem as though we are walking alone in the dark. Signs and symbols are in place: inside, beside, on and around us, guiding us to truth. But unless our energy is in keeping with our Higher Self, it is easy to dismiss them.

As always, maintaining balance will enable us to be spiritually aware, even during our most challenging circumstances. Remember, however, that exhaustion, doubt, frustration and fear, along with any other energy in opposition to truth, will make us wonder where Spirit is hiding.

Here is how Spirit reminded me to honor my truth.

With my permission, but without my awareness, I exchanged my old life for a foreign existence. Familiar rituals had been replaced by a new routine.

No longer was I leisurely sipping my morning coffee while recording insights in my journal. Now I was preparing formula, feeding my new baby and watching the 4 a.m. news. Daily walks around the block had been replaced by continually running up and down stairs in response to my baby's cries. Even my five-minute meditations had gone by the wayside, along with sleeping longer than three consecutive hours.

Like any 'new' mother, I was working non-stop. Entire weeks were passing by in a blur. I didn't know what hour it was. Sometimes I didn't know what day it was. More importantly, I didn't care. I was more than willing to make sacrifices for my new son. I could hardly believe he was real.

Exhaustion, however, was always there to remind me. Every moment of the day had my baby's name on it. If I wasn't feeding, changing or bathing him, I was making sure he was breathing while he slept. When I wasn't physically engaged with my baby, I was reading books on infant development – what to expect and when. It had been so long since I had given birth to my first son that I had to learn how to be a mother all over again.

Totally depleted, I focused on baby care. Thoroughly drained, I needed to address my own needs more than ever. Ironically, they were not even a consideration.

Time passed. More than a year went by. My baby was eagerly learning about his world. Meanwhile, having neglected to feed my soul, I began to forget all the lessons I thought I had learned.

Not only was I ignoring my spiritual self, but I was also acting as though that part of me didn't exist. I stopped reading and listening to anything inspirational. I wasn't writing anything other than shopping lists. Had it not been for my husband, who prepared wonderful dinners every night, I would have lived on crackers and peanut butter. Everything I did revolved around taking care of my family. Nothing I did had anything to do with me.

Knowing how unbalanced I had become, Spirit spoke up to tell me so. The truth came out of people I loved and trusted. My mother and sister encouraged me to get out of the house. Friends insisted that I take care of myself. My husband told me to make time for myself.

Unfortunately, there was so much noise in my life that I was unable to hear them. Spirit had no other alternative than to raise its voice.

It was two days before Easter and I had decided to make Easter eggs. Thomas was napping; I had time for myself. After piercing the top and bottom of each egg with a needle, I blew the contents out of its shell and into a bowl.

It was a cathartic experience – a long-overdue release of pent-up energies I had allowed to accumulate for over a year. The time passed quickly. It wasn't long before the baby awakened and started to cry.

On my way up the stairs, I happened to glance in the mirror. My reflection made me gasp; I was shocked at what I saw. Blowing out five eggs within two hours had a downside. Bruised from cheek to ear, I had broken blood vessels on the left half of my face.

Panicked, I remembered when my complexion had looked similar.

Ten years prior, I had been diagnosed with rosacea – a skin disorder that afflicts fair-skinned people, particularly women. On me, it had manifested as a butterfly-shaped expanse of inflamed pink and red blotches across my cheeks and nose. Although the dermatologist had attributed my condition to heat sensitivity and hormones, he admitted that very little was known about rosacea. Needing to understand it, I set out on a quest for truth.

At first, I chose the physical route and treated my symptoms with creams and medicines. I stayed out of the sun and stopped eating and drinking anything that could cause my face to flush. I noted how every product I used affected my skin. But my project had to be cut short; in the middle of my experiment I became pregnant. Medication was no longer an option.

During my pregnancy something amazing happened. My complexion gradually and mysteriously returned to normal – not even a hint of redness was apparent on my face. At the same time, I was happier and more at peace than ever before.

Unfortunately, I was oblivious to the connection.

Soon after my first son's birth, the rosacea returned, redder than ever. Although I didn't realize it then, Spirit had painted a picture on my skin, depicting feelings I was unable to express. Having lost my identity to the responsibilities of motherhood, I was wearing a mask made from sadness and fear.

It took many years before I was ready to hear Spirit's message. When my first son entered kindergarten, my healing began. For the first time in a long time, I made time to take care of myself; I learned how to feed my soul. As old patterns disappeared from my life, so did the rosacea.

Even though the present discoloration on my cheek had nothing to do with my former condition, looking at it now evoked the same dark feelings.

Eventually, the bruises began to fade. However, I was still holding onto the energy that had created them. As a result, redness began to appear on the other side of my face; the rosacea recurred.

Dissonant chaotic rhythms within me had resulted in an imbalance in my skin. Noise had arisen from where music had once played. I had allowed myself to become negative energy.

Spirit was telling me to feel the energy welling up inside me – to acknowledge the emotions that were trapped beneath my skin. I was too distracted by what I looked like to see the truth.

Meanwhile, as the noise level in my life escalated, redness took over my face. Not only was it on my cheeks, but three dark-red streaks had also appeared across my forehead.

It was as if someone had scribbled a message on me.

Unfortunately, fear had blinded me to the reality I had created; I was the one with the red marker in my hand. I had stopped taking care of myself. I had invited negativity back into my energy – disquieting my mind, unbalancing my body and disrupting my life.

Suddenly, I was reliving my past.

Negative, draining people I had long let go of started reappearing everywhere. Previous business acquaintances were finding me at the grocery store. Former clients were calling to see how much complimentary spiritual guidance they could obtain. Old friends were contacting me by phone or showing up unexpectedly at the door.

Everyone was as sad, depressed, frustrated and angry as the day I had originally said 'Goodbye'.

It was as if I was being forced to listen to a song I didn't like, over and over again, and someone kept increasing the volume. I didn't believe in coincidences and I knew there were no such things as accidents. I believed everything happened for a reason. But I had no clue as to what it could be.

That didn't stop Spirit from whispering the truth to me.

Any moment of quiet offered my Higher Self an opportunity to speak. One Sunday, I turned on the TV to hear an evangelist at the end of his sermon say, 'Bring peace into your life if it's the only thing you are able to do.' That same day, I went for a walk to meditate, and a song about truth I had never heard before played in my head. Afterward, something I had once written fell out of my notebook. It read, 'We are responsible for creating our own reality.'

From then on, I made sure to take care of myself. Feeding my soul became my first priority. I started taking long walks. I spent time with positive people. I wrote in my journal. I made time for peace.

Gradually, as I improved the condition of my life, I improved the condition of my skin. My red complexion faded when I reclaimed my true identity. It healed when I faced the truth.

***

During the transition process, Spirit illuminates an old issue to provide us with the opportunity to view it from a higher perspective. We may re-experience a physical or emotional imbalance, relationship conflict, or financial hardship. Things we thought we had overcome resurface so we can understand their true spiritual meaning.

Our old issues may resurface for many reasons. Maybe we have forgotten our lessons and need a refresher course. Maybe we know them but have neglected to apply them to our life. Perhaps we are trying to determine whether or not we are ready to make the lessons we have learned a permanent part of our soul. Or possibly, Spirit is simply offering us a choice: to accept the illusion of our circumstances as truth, or trust the truth behind the illusion.

More than ever before, it is of utmost importance that we take good care of ourselves. Exhaustion, thinking negative thoughts and neglecting to feed our souls will predispose us to falling back into old patterns. At the same time, our energy will make us prone to inviting disquieting energies into our life. Balancing ourselves through meditation and nurturing ourselves in every possible way will continually remind us that Spirit is ever-present within us.

Remember, Spirit has our answers. As long as we remain true to ourselves, we are prepared to pass whatever tests we are given.

Transition time is when we have swept our house clean and Spirit shines light on the dust we didn't see behind the couch. It is when we take one last walk through our old neighborhood before we say 'Goodbye'. It is when we see the road ahead and wonder how far we have yet to go, only to look over our shoulder to realize just how far we have come.

Chapter 9

Truth

Cramming my belongings into a suitcase and stuffing my fears deep inside me, I decided to bury my past. Kent State was only hours away; my new life awaited me. No one would know who I was, or more importantly, who I used to be.

It was an empowering decision: erasing years of yesterdays, pretending the past never happened or that it happened to someone else. College was about to start; my old life was over. The memories, however, were still alive.

I don't know exactly when Lisa Martini first beat me up at the bus stop and I never understood why. But for no apparent reason she attacked me. Out of a half-dozen kids, she had singled me out. It was as if we had signed a contract to act in a long-running nightmarish play. From grade school to high school, Lisa was the bully and I was her victim.

The abuse was relentless. It began the moment I reached the bus stop and didn't end until the bus arrived. First, Lisa teased me and I ignored her. Then she shoved, hit and kicked me until I cried.

While bruises, cuts and scrapes were visible on my body, Lisa's parents, two school teachers, pretended not to notice. Even with my mother standing by my side, they downplayed what their daughter had done to me. 'Teasing is part of growing up,' they said. 'Robin needs to learn how to fight her own battles.'

Not only did the abuse continue, but it also worsened over time. There was no reasoning with Lisa. She had no interest in working out whatever was wrong between us. She seemed to derive pleasure out of mentally and physically torturing me.

I tried everything to make her stop. Ignoring her didn't work;

it made her want to hurt me more. Fighting back didn't accomplish anything except to make her angry. Waiting until the last minute to walk to the bus stop didn't help either. There was still enough time for her to express mean-spiritedness toward me in some way.

My mother saw everything that was happening to me. Our house was across the street from the bus stop, so she had a good view. Mom was continually rescuing me. If she wasn't confronting Lisa and her parents over the phone, she was reporting in person every abuse she had seen their daughter commit. She continued doing so, until the day they stopped talking to her.

For years, getting slapped, pushed around or thrown into the driveway was how most of my school days began. As sad as it is to admit, I got used to the pain. It was humiliating to be physically assaulted while my peers watched. But what hurt more were the words Lisa used to slice my soul.

'You're ugly! You're stupid! Nobody likes you!' She would say it more and more loudly, faster and faster, over and over again. Then she invited others to repeat her words. It was a horrible chant – something my heart held and my mind memorized. It was a description I believed defined me – a lie I mistook for truth.

Lisa Martini wasn't my only bully. There were many others. Physical and verbal abuse followed me practically everywhere – on the bus, in the classroom and in the cafeteria. As early as first grade, a classmate seared my arm on a radiator. Throughout grade school, she and others like her were continually invading my space. Once, in sixth grade during recess, a group of classmates held me upside down on a seesaw, ripped off my clothes and collectively groped me. Their laughter hurt me far more than the physical violation.

From then on, trusting people was difficult for me. I had a small circle of friends. But as far as I knew, they were just pretending to enjoy my company. I believed that it would only be a matter of time before they hurt me.

By the time I reached high school, the physical abuse had ended. But hurtful words continued to be hurled in my direction. The last humiliating school experience I can recall happened in tenth grade. I was walking down a hallway where athletes leaned on the wall and 'rated' every girl that passed by. My name was announced, followed by a negative number.

After that, there were no more bullies to fear. However, I had become adept at emotionally beating myself up. Even when the braces on my teeth had been removed and my dark curly hair had grown long, I criticized and judged what I saw in the mirror. In my eyes, I was ugly. My reflection was a lie.

Having been programmed for abuse, I unknowingly began seeking it out. Throughout high school, in college and afterward, if someone wasn't hurting me in some way, I made sure to mentally, emotionally or physically inflict pain upon myself.

I attracted boyfriends with the same energy but a different face. I would let them use me, disrespect me and mistreat me. I became promiscuous – mistaking sex for love. I developed an eating disorder, alternating anorexic behavior with overeating – losing and gaining 25 pounds, on and off for a decade. I became agoraphobic, had almost daily panic attacks and was almost always depressed.

Keeping people at a distance became my life's theme. If they weren't close, they couldn't hurt me. I avoided social situations for fear of being judged and didn't drive for the same reason. I never let anyone see me without makeup, believing I was unlovable without it. I sabotaged anything good that tried to come into my life, believing I didn't deserve it.

Even after being a DJ for my own college radio show and graduating from college with a B.A. degree in communications, I lacked the confidence to pursue a communications-related career. I didn't believe I was good enough.

Six years later, I married. Two years afterward, I became a mother for the first time. But it wasn't until I began my work as a spiritual healer that my shattered soul began to mend. Offering spiritual direction to others, and lighting their way with love, compassion and understanding, empowered me to heal myself.

I identified with their pain – the abuses they had allowed to obliterate their truths. I understood their inability to love themselves and trust others. Not only had I walked that road, but I had also worn those shoes. In fact, I had worn them out. As Spirit's voice spoke through me, explaining to my clients where they were, why they were there and how they could get to a better place, I knew the advice I was offering was not just for them.

Slowly, I started to heal all of me – to take care of myself on all levels of being. It was a lengthy process – a series of spiritual challenges designed to teach me my truth.

One by one, I peeled off the layers of lies I had been wearing for a lifetime. I fell apart, picked up the pieces and put myself together, again and again and again. Eventually, I realized that nothing was ever missing – that Spirit is always with me. But not until I had learned that lesson from every angle, inside and out, upside down and while standing on my head, did I finally 'get it'. When I did, it completely transformed my life.

It took years to learn how to love myself unconditionally. It took patience to reprogram my mind in a positive way. Little by little, I did whatever I needed to do to heal. I stopped putting myself down and started practicing self-respect. I believed I deserved to attract people and circumstances that supported me. In turn, they found me. I trusted light to pour into my life and, in time, it did.

***

Embarking upon a spiritual journey is signing a contract to

honor truth. Each step we take offers us the opportunity to better understand our true identity – to become more deeply aware of who we really are. Each experience we have invites us to examine life through Spirit's microscope and magnifying glass. Each soul we meet not only asks us to look in the mirror, but also to study our reflection in the light.

When we embrace Spirit, we know the difference between truth and illusion – who we are versus what we do and what we own. While our career, bank account, car, clothes and home may reflect our energy, we are aware that things do not define us. We know our life force is our true signature – the light within that shines through to the world. As the energy of truth, we cannot lie if we try; the universe won't permit it. Living in the light means we can see the spiritual stories beneath our physical circumstances. We understand what they mean.

No longer can we look the other way. Truth is wherever we are. It lives in our spirit, mind and body. It flows from our thoughts into the physical world. It is the basis from which we build our reality – the one that supports our soul.

When we close our eyes, truth finds us in our dreams. When we open them, it is everywhere we look: on the license plate in front of us, in the supermarket checkout line and on the back of a teenager's T-shirt in big, bold letters.

We hear Spirit offering us wisdom, compassion and kindness in our best friend's voice. When we do the same for others, we know our Higher Self is speaking. We feel truth whenever chills tingle our spine, inexplicable warmth wraps itself around us from nowhere, or we receive that special signal – the one that means *Pay attention: this is important and this is true.*

One spiritual transformation after another has caused us to shed layers of untruths – lies we believed were true. The more lessons we have learned, the more light we are, the more truth we know.

There are no mistakes. There are no accidents. There are no

coincidences. Everything happens for a reason. We can pretend that our two cars with dead batteries in the driveway have no connection whatsoever to us, and that the illness that has sent us to bed at the same time has nothing to do with our total state of being. But the truth is that we know both events hold meaning. As for the dream we have just had about being hospitalized for back surgery, maybe we should consider its symbolic significance as well. All signs are pointing to a truth we cannot ignore: our batteries need to be recharged, because we're exhausted and we're carrying too much on our back.

Conducting life in the dark is no longer possible with the light on. Spirit is making us acutely aware of our answers – whatever we need to know. As truth, we are light. If we try to invite anything into our life that is not for our Highest Good, we will soon learn that doing so is not an option.

Now, having just one negative thought will create immediate repercussions on all levels of being. It will feel wrong to think ill of anyone or anything, to judge, criticize, disrespect, dishonor or abuse oneself or others. In addition, holding onto that thought will not only disquiet our mind but will also lead to emotional upset such as sadness, frustration and anger. Furthermore, as a result of the negativity we are carrying, physical symptoms of imbalance will appear, notifying us that we're walking down a dark, hazardous road.

Despite Spirit's repeated warnings, if we insist on thinking and acting according to our 'old self', the universe will make us stop, force us to be quiet, and redirect us to safe and solid ground.

Here is the story of how Spirit showed me the way.

It was Valentine's Day and I was taking a walk. The morning air was almost too cold to breathe. But I needed to find peace. I wanted Spirit to find me, so I kept walking.

I had forgotten what it felt like to be quiet. For more than a year, I had been living in noise. Ever since Thomas had learned to walk, I had been running after him. From the moment he awoke until the time he went to bed, my son was in motion. Naps were rare; temper tantrums happened every day.

Thomas was my mirror. Unfortunately, it was too dark for me to see the truth. I had stopped feeding my soul.

Even in the bitter cold, it felt good to be outside. The street was quiet. The neighborhood was still. I couldn't remember the last time I had taken a walk by myself. I had forgotten how much I loved to be outdoors. Walking gave me peace. It was the way I connected with Spirit.

As I turned the corner, I saw a sheet of ice in front of me. Alongside it was a strip of snow. I had a choice. Either I could head down the treacherous path. Or I could walk where it was safe. It was my decision.

I stepped off the sidewalk into the snow and continued walking. As I walked, I prayed. I asked Spirit for guidance.

Moments later, comforting words began to fill my mind. At the same time, an unfamiliar melody 'played' from somewhere deep within me.

Nothing like this had ever happened before.

I wanted to write down the words so I could remember them. But I didn't have anything to write with. Aside from that, I didn't know how to write music.

Spirit had given me a gift – words of wisdom to guide me and music to heal my soul. The only thing I could do was memorize the song that had been whispered to me. I hummed the tune. I recited the words. I sang the song over and over again. By the time I stepped foot in my driveway, I knew it by heart.

My family was waiting for me in the kitchen; there was a bouquet of flowers on the table. The boys were hungry so I made them their favorite breakfasts. Jp asked for toast and an egg, sunny-side up. Thomas requested a giant pancake.

I cracked the egg into one pan and poured pancake batter into the other. While everything was cooking, I wrote down 'my' song. I returned to the stove, knowing Spirit was with me. When I looked into the pans, I started to cry.

The yolk on Jp's egg had broken in the shape of a heart. Thomas's pancake had turned into a heart as well.

***

Where Truth Resides (The Song)

Spirit is alive inside you
Trust the light inside to guide you
Embrace the place within your soul
That knows the truth that makes you whole
See yourself inside the mirror
Look beyond your pain and fear
Then close your eyes and clear your mind
Get past your thoughts and you will find
The answers to your questions – the path to your life's dream
Your world of possibilities is closer than it seems
Forget your cares and worries, the troubles in your mind
Forget what others tell you; you know the truth inside
Just keep on walking through the night
Just keep your focus on the light
The road ahead is clear to see
Just trust your heart to set you free
You know the way; you know the road
Forget the lies that you've been told
Just close your eyes and you will know
Just hear the whisper of your soul
Just hear the whisper of your soul
Just hear the whisper of your soul
Just hear the whisper.

When our soul is peaceful, our heart is open and our mind is still. We are ready and willing to embrace truth. We trust what is happening within and around us. We trust that Spirit will tell us what it really means – that, in time, we will become aware of the answer we already know.

At the same time, the things we no longer desire to own show themselves to us, so we may name them, face them and send them away with love. This allows us to walk into the present, unencumbered by the weight of the past.

The most powerful messages can arise when we least expect them. In this breathtaking moment of truth, Spirit showed me exactly what I needed to see.

***

I did my best to console Thomas. He couldn't stop crying. I stroked his hair. I kissed his forehead. I whispered that everything was going to be all right. But none of my efforts were making a difference. He was unaware of my presence in all the noise.

Thomas had called '9ll' hours before. He had pulled a prank on his older brother. Jp hadn't wanted to play with him. Thomas had threatened to call the police if he didn't change his mind. Thomas had just apologized. I had forgiven him. The officers who responded to his call had forgiven him as well.

There was just one problem. My son wasn't ready to forgive himself.

Thomas kept talking about what had happened. He insisted on beating himself up over what he had done. Over and over again, he was reliving the incident. Even as he was falling asleep Thomas was saying, 'I'm sorry.' Kissing him, I told him that the past was over; it was time to move on.

Suddenly the room was silent. In quiet, I focused on my little boy. I looked at him. I studied him. I saw the truth in him; I saw myself in him. Thomas was my reflection in disguise.

While I watched him sleeping, questions came to mind.

'How often do I revisit the past? How many times do I think about something I have done, wishing it had never happened or that I could do it over again? When will I be ready to forgive myself?'

With tears in my eyes, I prayed. I held one hand with the other to remind myself that I wasn't alone. I took long, slow, deep breaths. When I exhaled, I focused on letting go of anything I was holding onto – everything from the argument that happened at breakfast to the abuse I had experienced as a child.

It was a life-changing moment. Not only did I feel the presence of my Higher Self, but I also understood the meaning of 'oneness'. As I handed Spirit every dark, heavy thing I had been holding, I felt lighter. I knew the meaning of 'letting go'.

***

Imagine: We are standing in the here and now, turning around to look at yesterday – knowing we can no longer live there. At the same time, the bridge we have crossed to get from there to here has disintegrated. Now, even if we wanted it, there is no way back to where we came from or who we used to be.

We could try to hike there, but our old path is overgrown with thorny weeds. We could try navigating our way by boat, but the current is flowing in the opposite direction. We could try to fly there, but there is no safe place to land.

In this moment, we realize that all we can do is view from a distance what once was – to see how far we have come, how much we have grown. The past has passed. We have left our pain and fears there, along with every other negative vibration we once believed we owned – the things we allowed to weigh us down, anchor us in place and prevent us from moving forward.

Now, we are holding onto the lessons we have learned within

the light we have become from having learned them. And as my insightful mother reminds us, if ever we are tempted to step into the old neighborhood where we used to live, we only have to look at our footprints to realize that we are headed in the wrong direction. For once we have made the commitment to honor our truth, there is no turning back.

The road to truth is the path of enlightenment. The more we walk, the more we learn. The more light-filled we become, the more light we can shine on each other, the world and the universe. Little by little, as life's details are illuminated, we recognize the divine within them. We know their meaning.

Spirit speaks; we listen. As we allow intuition to guide us through each day, we know we are standing in the right place at the right time and that our feet are pointed in the right direction. We know our answers are within – that searching for them elsewhere will only lead us back to ourselves.

BOOKS

MySpiritRadio